CW00872195

The Secret Life of EL James

an unauthorized biography

Marc Shapiro

For more information, address
Riverdale Avenue Books
5676 Riverdale Avenue
Riverdale, NY 10471.

www.riverdaleavebooks.com

Design by www.formatting4U.com
Cover by Scott Carpenter

Digital ISBN 9781626010017
Print ISBN   9781626010000

Second Edition February 2015

TABLE OF CONTENTS

THIS BOOK IS DEDICATED TO...

My wife Nancy, my daughter Rachael, my granddaughter Lily. Brady and Fitch. Mike. Lori Perkins. The exciting new adventure that is Riverdale Avenue Books. As always good books, good art and good music. All the things real and imagined that get us through the days and nights. The wins we revel in and the losses we learn from. No moment is wasted. E L James has the right idea.

INTRODUCTION
WOMEN OF A CERTAIN AGE

Middle-aged housewives and mothers. Girls barely out of their teens.

Grandmothers. Blindfolds. Restraints. Dominance. Submission.

Sadomasochism. What's wrong with this picture?

Absolutely nothing thanks to E L James, a middle-aged, hard-working British wife and mother who has single-handedly succeeded in bringing erotica kicking and screaming to a heretofore unheard of level of acceptance and freedom with her trilogy of sexually charged *Fifty Shades* novels.

Fifty Shades of Grey. Fifty Shades Darker. Fifty Shades Freed. The titles ring out like a call to arms. The battle ultimately won has been for the freedom for women to think and feel.

Fifty Shades books are proudly displayed, in stacks many feet high, in bookstore displays around the world. They've made the leap from fan fiction homage to the *Twilight* series to best-seller status in a much more adult world at light speed.

And far from the days of back of the store/brown paper wrapper book covers secured and digested in hushed tones that greeted forerunners of the modern erotic novel like *Lady Chatterley's Lover, The Story of O, Peyton Place (*very hot stuff for its day), *Fanny Hill, Fear of Flying* and the more erotic writing of Anais Nin and, more recently, Anne Rice, fans of these very raw romantic and sexual odysseys are proudly and openly displaying their books, discussing them in very public arenas. In the ultimate sign of respectability, these books can be purchased in Aisle 4 of their favorite supermarket from mile-high displays next to the frozen food cases, as well as in front-of-the-store displays normally reserved for what many would consider more serious forms of literature as well as the latest efforts of the best-seller brands.

You know that erotica has truly arrived when you can buy *Fifty Shades of Grey* and creamed corn in the same place.

This is a classic case of "where did this come from?" We've seen it before with the series by J.K. Rowling and Stephenie Meyer. Yes, E L James has quickly risen to that level of company and, as such, is reaping the rewards.

Not surprisingly, a spirited bidding war for the film rights to *Fifty Shades* ensued in 2012 with major film studios falling all over themselves to the tune of millions of dollars. Even actress Angelina Jolie has tossed her hat into the ring to direct while author Bret Easton Ellis, who has had his own share of controversy with *American Psycho*, has enthusiastically lobbied to adapt the books for the screen.

BDSM merchandise has escaped the dungeons of kinky specialty shops and is flying out the door of above ground, mainstream department stores. And let's not forget the soundtrack albums, the fuzzy handcuffs and all the trappings of an underground movement that has risen to ground level on the back of one middle-aged housewife and one very graphic love story. It has all the elements of an out-of-nowhere success story that has been a happy ending literally from the word go.

This success has been made all the more amazing by the fact that E L James' creation is, at its core, fairly predictable stuff by erotic standards.

The conceit of *Fifty Shades'* story is fairly traditional. An inexperienced young woman named Anastasia Steele becomes involved with an older and light years more experienced man, billionaire Christian Grey, who teaches her the ways of life and love. It is your basic romance novel, the ones with the strapping male torsos and the willowy women cowering at their feet.

So far so good.

But where the *Fifty Shades* books have radically departed from the polite/well mannered norm of mass-market romance paperbacks is that the older man in this scenario has a few kinks. He is into control and dominance when it comes to his lovers, be it in or out of his notorious Red Room of Pain. Sadomasochism is part and parcel of his lovemaking. Handcuffs, whips, blindfolds and bindings are integral to his foreplay. Control is at the center of this erotic dance. Who has it? Who is willing to accept it?

And finally, who says when it's all too much?

And make no mistake, James does not pull any punches with the sexual nature of the couple's encounters. Hardcore and rude in the typical pornographic manner, it is not. But the descriptive and truly erotic passages offer just the right element of unbridled heat and passion. Readers are quick to turn the pages ... for all the right and wrong reasons.

And women of all ages and, particularly, James' middle-aged peers who had, according to pop culture pundits looking to make sense of *Fifty Shades*, admittedly fallen into a sedate state of routine and, yes, perhaps boredom in their love lives, have literally been drawn to the flame of this later-in-life fictional experience. And for many reasons.

Many have speculated that *Fifty Shades* is a mirror on the excitement of long-ago first love. Others offer up the tales as the fantasy many women crave of being dominated by a strong man; their escape from a workaday world that often sees them as the breadwinner and competing in a male-driven society. For still others, Christian is the erotic one-night stand they dream of when the husband or significant other has fallen asleep and the children are off in their own lives. Pundits have had a field day trying to figure it all out. But at the end of the day, the attraction to *Fifty Shades* has been undeniable.

One enthusiastic convert to the allure of the *Fifty Shades* trilogy summed things up fairly succinctly when she sent James a note (chronicled in *The Daily Mail*) informing her that the effect of the books on her readers was as though "you're waking the dead here."

While wildly successful on a massive commercial scale, the odyssey of Christian and Anastasia has not gone by unscathed. James herself has often made the point that she is not a great writer and, inevitably, that point is made even in the most complimentary reviews. Take away the erotic passages and most would find the storyline fairly suitable fodder for generic romance novels.

As they would likely find the company of E L James (the nom de plume of former British television producer Erika Leonard). This late-40s mother of two is alternately soft-spoken and self-deprecating. After years of a solid family life with no bumps in the road, she experienced what she calls "her midlife crisis" that resulted in the creation of *Fifty Shades* and a level of fame that she constantly marvels at and, even at this late date, still finds hard to believe. To put it mildly, she was "gobsmacked."

As a matter of fact, amazement at it all has become James' stock answer to the endless questions of how sudden success and riches beyond her wildest dreams feels. The plain spoken, to the point and slightly understated responses to just how success feels are refreshingly obvious and have taken on a life of their own. How many ways can you describe how it feels to suddenly have it all? E L James has a million of them and, to this point, has used them all. Including a rather understated response to NPR during an interview. "My name is E L James. I'm in my 40s and I do lots of laundry... And write books."

James' mother, Alexandra Mitchell, echoed her daughter's surprise at the books' success in an Entertainmentwise interview. "It was a lovely surprise. None of us expected it. She didn't either. She was writing it for herself. She didn't even want to publish it at first. She said to me, 'I never wanted to be a famous mother.'"

To that point, James was visibly upset when *The London Evening Standard* saw through her E L James pseudonym and tracked her down at her quiet, nondescript West London home. "How did you find me?" she asked the journalist who came knocking on her door. "I didn't want my real name to come out."

Nor did she have high expectations when the very small publisher, The Writer's Coffee Shop, began publishing her books. "I thought I would put it out, get a few gentle sales and I'd carry on with my work," she told the New Zealand news website stuff.co.nz.

Not surprisingly, when *Fifty Shades* became an international sensation, James, as given her modest roots, proclaimed that she would use the money to buy a new car and fix up her kitchen. But, as she explained in quotes that appeared in *The Daily Mail* and Face The Facts, she did make one subtle concession to her erotic alter ego.

"I bought some made-to-measure bras," she chuckled. "They're very plain. They haven't got tassels or anything raunchy on them."

That James' modest/low-key traits sound vaguely familiar come as no surprise. For James is the latest in a long line of midlife women writers who after years of quiet obscurity have had mammoth, unexpected breakthroughs. We've seen it with J.K. Rowling who, after years of personal and creative challenges and frustrations, made literary history with *Harry Potter*. Stephenie Meyer, for whom James owes a real sense of gratitude and inspiration, lived a prim and proper life in Middle American bliss before a dream resulted in *Twilight*.

But as the accolades and book sales came pouring

in, reaching their peak in early 2012 with an estimated one million copies sold a week, James began to loosen up. She became more comfortable in the public eye, laughed easily and often in the face of inquiring press and adoring fans, and developed a quite easy and believable patter during her first U.S. book tour.

During a stopover in Chicago, as reported by *The Chicago Tribune*, she was alternately shy and forthcoming. She visibly blushed at one point when an ardent fan relayed a personal thank you from her husband. When another woman told her that she was now very pregnant thanks to her, James jokingly responded, "I never touched you."

James' dream has become the lightning rod of a sudden realization that love and sex as a freedom for bottled-up emotions and fantasies can be possible. Pop culture being what it is, those who make a living defining something at its most basic have been quick to call what E L James has written "Mommy porn."

James has had a good laugh at the notion of her work being dismissed as porn or something equally scandalous. To her way of thinking, even the more civilized "erotica" is missing the boat.

"I wouldn't call it erotica," she told Stuff. "I call it a contemporary romance. What's in my books is what people do. They meet, fall in love and have sex. That's what I remember from back in the day."

CHAPTER ONE
BORN AND RAISED

It would not be too difficult to fall in love with Buckinghamshire. Surrounded by rolling hills, idyllic country sides and crisscrossed by lazy, meandering rivers that cross hatch the various counties in South Eastern England, Buckinghamshire is nothing if not gentile. The service-oriented economy of the city is backed by the highest level of educational achievement in the United Kingdom. Numerous British celebrities hail from Buckinghamshire, including '80s pop singer Howard Jones, actor Michael York, and five-time Olympic gold medalist Steve Redgrave. During medieval times, no lesser lights than Edward the Confessor and Ann Boleyn made Buckinghamshire their home.

It was the place where Erika Leonard's parents put down roots, mixing their Scottish and Chilean backgrounds and an abiding interest in the finer, creative elements of life into the fabric of the town. Her father plied his trade in the big city as a cameraman for the BBC while her mother tended home and hearth.

For whatever reason, the particulars of Erika's

family tree are maddeningly inconsistent. Whether by design or the relative privacy of the author, research has failed to disclose her father's name. It was only within the past year and a chance interview with her mother (Alexandra) and the occasional memories of the author that we discovered precious fragments of those early years, such as the fact that she has a brother.

Erika Leonard was born in Buckinghamshire in 1963. From the beginning, it seemed like a good fit.

While very much stepped in tradition, Erika's parents raised their daughter with a soft, encouraging hand. At an early age, Erika was quite naturally bilingual, speaking fluid Spanish along with a very crisp British lilt. Very much a self-described "good girl," the young Erika was equally at home with friends and in the privacy of her own imagination and thoughts. When out and about, she could often be counted on for the amusing anecdote or off-the-cuff remark that could induce mild surprise and laughter. She recalled in an interview with romance author journalist Rachael Wade that a sense of humor was a family trait.

"My father and brother both had and have an amazing sense of humor," she said. "My mother has a tremendous sense of mischief. So it kind of rubbed off."

It was a trait of mild outlandishness that would follow her throughout the years.

"I've always had a tendency to over-share," she jokingly explained in a *Times of India* article. "I'm not a particularly reserved person."

The young child grew up in a house of readers

and gravitated toward a love of the written word, and by the time she entered school, she was already making tentative strides in composing flights of fancy to entertain herself and her classmates.

"When I was in primary school at age 10, I used to write stories," she told Fiction Vixen. "My teacher would always make me read them to the class. That was mainly because I used to include my classmates in every story."

James' mother, Alexandra Mitchell, proudly recalled her daughter's earliest writing efforts in a conversation with *The Daily Mail*. "Erika won't remember this, but she wrote something that was absolutely brilliant about a snowman that flew."

The notion of writing stories that would center on love and captivate the hearts and minds of massive audiences was part and parcel of Erika's early years.

Erika's childhood and teen years were normal by most standards. She played hard. She studied hard. And she stayed out of trouble. By the time she finished up her primary education, the consensus was that Erika Mitchell would be going places.

CHAPTER TWO
HIGHER EDUCATION

Erika's interests were running very much toward the intellectual side when it came time for her to go onto the next phase of her education life. Ultimately she chose to attend the prestigious University of Kent with a major in History, filled out by classes in English Literature.

Her years at Kent must have seemed to have flown by. Alternately studious and outgoing, Erika remained personable in social settings and dedicated in her studies. On the surface, a career in teaching seemed the logical career path. And although she remained enamored of the idea of writing stories and, reportedly, would produce occasional bits and fragments of short stories that never saw the light of day, a career as a woman of letters did not appear to be on the horizon.

What is known about Erika during this period was that she was very detail-oriented, good with numbers and highly organized. Given that aptitude, it was no surprise that her final dissertation at the university was a complex and detailed look at the fall of the Tsar of Russia. It was a paper that earned Erika high marks.

And it was safe to say that Erika's father had some input when it came to discussing what his daughter might do once she graduated from university. He would most likely have played up the excitement of being in the entertainment industry and Erika would have been taken with the notion of a career in a creative world.

Which was why it did not come as too much of a surprise when, despite having graduated from the University of Kent with a degree in History, Erika turned toward entertainment when she applied to and was accepted at the prestigious National Film and Television School in London. The school had a sterling reputation as a real world entry into show business thanks to its mixture of education and theory, as well as lots of on-the-job training.

Erika's personal life during this period remained a deep-dark secret. But during her U.S. book tour, she did let it slip that, "I did have an inappropriate relationship when I was younger." She would not be any more specific. But the speculation ran wild with the notion that this relationship, rumored to have happened sometime after she graduated from Kent and during her early years at The National Film and Television School, may well have planted the seeds, on a subconscious level, for the domineering Christian Grey in *Fifty Shades*.

Erika was thrown into the deep end at The National Film and Television School, serving as the studio manager's assistant, essentially a gofer who did anything and everything and learned quite a bit along the way. It was a tough and constantly challenging exercise in on-the-job training but Erika was not deterred by the nuts and bolts nature of this new element of her education.

While at the school, Erika met a fellow student, Niall Leonard, a good-natured Irishman with a sly sense of humor and a very down-to-earth nature. That he was a creative type who was pointing toward a career as a scriptwriter and director was of particular interest to Erika. And their friendship soon blossomed into something more.

Becoming romantically involved proved to be quite a natural and easygoing scenario for the pair. Niall was making his first forays into writing and directing while Erika was proving her mettle with all the bottom-line skills and instincts of a seasoned producer. They both had their work and education. And when they were together they were genuinely excited by each other and their lives. Niall was never what one would consider a romantic. He made that plain in a *Guardian* commentary when he talked about his seeming inability to write a romantic novel. "I'm the least romantic fecker that ever lived. Our first Christmas together I bought her a tin opener. My earliest experience of kinky sex was her trying to shove it up my arse."

"We annoy the hell out of each other," Erika jokingly revealed about the nature of their relationship to Irish Central. "But generally, we get on very well."

So well, in fact, that they made their life together permanent when they married in 1987.

The couple settled into marital bliss in a nondescript home in a quiet area of West London. The early years were a whirlwind as they moved ahead in their education and made the first tentative steps forward in their respective careers.

But as these things often happen, Erika adjusted quite easily to the role of a stay-at-home housewife who enjoyed the simple pleasures of puttering around in a small garden and being the doting wife. When she had a few moments to herself, Erika would curl up with a good book. Always an avid reader, those days she gravitated toward romance novels and an escape into fantasy.

In the meantime, Niall's growing reputation as a screenwriter had made him an in-demand writer on a number of the BBC's growing roster of television series. He would be kept busy over the next few years on the shows *Spender* (1993), *Pie In The Sky* (1997) and *Ballykissangel* (1997-1998).

The marriage took a happy turn when Erika discovered that she was pregnant in 1991. The couple's first child, a boy, was born in 1992. Erika and Niall were beside themselves with happiness and Erika was nothing if not the ideal mother. And even more in love with Niall.

"My husband is a wonderful man," she told a boston.com interviewer. "He's a very real man."

As the days and months passed by, the idea of motherhood and a large family was so much on their minds that, two years later, they would welcome a second child, another boy, into the world.

The ensuing years were idyllic for the young couple. They were content with their stature in suburban middle class London, very much the equivalent of low-key luxury. She drove a Mini Cooper. Her favorite drink was Oyster Bay sauvignon blanc, which cost a hefty 8 pounds a bottle. On the personal front, she has candidly offered that she is not a morning person and that her husband snored.

"I was the only woman in the house," she laughingly confided to Bona Fide Reflections. "I lived with four men; a grumpy old Irishman (her husband), two teenagers, a West Highland Terrier named Max and, for the longest time, a hamster named Chewy."

But as the children grew and the years moved on, Erika found herself growing restless. She wanted to work, and with Niall primarily working at home when writing scripts, when the boys weren't in primary school, her children would be looked after.

And while marriage and motherhood had made her forget about writing, Erika was never far from a good book.

"I used to read all sorts of different things," she told a miami.com interviewer. "I belonged to various book clubs."

Inevitably she was drawn to romance fiction, her way of escaping the workaday life and, at least for a while, into a world of pure fantasy. Erika grew particularly fond of the romance writers Elizabeth Lowell, Laura Kinsale and Judith McNaught.

Niall had always been loving and supportive of his wife's desires and so, when the subject of her taking a job was broached, he was quick to encourage her.

And so by 1999, Erika was back out in the working world.

CHAPTER THREE
ALL WORK AND NO PLAY

Niall's working relationship with the BBC had always been very good. So it seemed like a good idea for Erika to take her first foray into the employment world to the hallowed halls of the British Broadcasting Corporation.

Erika was most likely a bundle of nerves and excitement as she boarded the tube that would take her into the heart of London. The BBC was legendary for having a never-ending array of creative outlets in television, radio, films and documentaries. There would almost certainly be a place for Erika.

Erika's penchant for organization and numbers was rewarded with an appointment to the position of production executive for the BBC comedy series *Funny Turns*. Erika's duties on the show involved the logistics of contracts, budgets and licensing. "I have only worked in television," she related to Bona Fide Reflections. "I have done everything from live music to dramas to documentaries."

What would appear mundane and boring to many fit right in with Erika's penchant for detail. The job lasted until the year 2000. With so many properties,

Erika was soon onto another job within the organization; production executive on the television movie *Goodbye 2000*, which, in turn, led to a similar production position on the television documentary *There's Only One Madonna*.

During a London speaking engagement, James disclosed a brief history of her work in the television industry. "I worked for 412 years in TV," she joked. "Yes, I'm one of the undead. I started life at The National School of Film and Television. Then I started working in the independent sector, then changed and started working at the BBC. I went into entertainment and music, that sort of thing. I had a great time actually. It was fantastic."

While she enjoyed her work and the idea of being out and about in the world, James confessed in a Fiction Vixens interview that there were those days when things did not look so ideal.

"For a long time, I was working from an office in the center of London. It was a high pressure, stressful job."

Entering the workaday world also increased Erika's penchant for reading. The sheer challenge of being a working wife and mother had cut her leisure reading time to almost nothing. But, as she recalled in an interview with miami.com, the ride to and from downtown London afforded her the opportunity to once again turn a page.

"The commute to work on the Underground was such a miserable journey. I would use the time on the tube to escape into whatever I could find."

The now defunct Murder One Bookshop on Charring Cross Road became a regular stopover for

Erika's never-ending search for new reading material. Primarily a source for mysteries and thrillers, Murder One also did a thriving business in the imports of U.S. romance novels. Erika wandered into the romance section one day and became entranced by the colorful and splashy covers that promised romance and escape.

More often than not, what she was finding were that the romance novels she now purchased on a regular basis, many of which had adult-themed stories and somewhat risqué covers, were taking her to a place of comfort and escape; a place that was far removed from the hustle and bustle of big city life. Erika became hooked on the stories of fantasy romance but was a bit embarrassed, should any of her co-riders see what she was reading.

"I'd have to bend the book covers back so no one would see them," she told miami.com. "I'm not keen on those kinds of covers with torsos all over them."

But over the course of her daily rides to work, she would succeed in racing through several books a week. Books by Catherine Coulter, Heather Graham and Karen Robards would come and go to the "read" pile in a matter of days. She would later admit that stacks of romance novels numbering into the hundreds were taking up space in a rarely entered room of her house.

Erika's fondness for romance novels was very public knowledge to her co-workers. During breaks in the day, they would often find her in a chair in a faraway corner, her nose buried in a book. "I often took a ribbing when people saw whatever novel I was reading," she explained to My Secret Romance.

Erika would move seamlessly between assignments. But she was still very much the homebody, rushing home on the tube after a day of juggling numbers to be with her boys and her husband. Ever the level-headed one, Erika would good-naturedly deflect any notion that she was working in the glamorous entertainment industry. She knew her place in the show business pipeline. She was a numbers cruncher, pure and simple.

But she had developed a certain fascination with all the behind-the-scenes machinations required to put a successful show on the air. And she had always made a point of being at home when the important steps in her children's lives took place. Happily she had not missed a thing.

Given the nature of television, Erika's job description was largely transitory. Consequently, over the next few years, she was essentially on call to direct the nuts and bolts of several BBC and outside production offerings. She contributed her skills to the 2002 comedy short *Not Another Eurovision Song Contest*. In 2003, she laid the budgetary and contractual groundwork for the series *Have I Got News For You*, a show she would return to sporadically until 2006. She would serve in production executive positions on two television series in 2004, *Bodies* and *Room 101*, before jumping behind the scenes for the Vodafone Live Music Awards in 2006.

However, by 2007, Erika found herself with a bad case of the blues. The grind she felt on the job weighed heavily on her and, she later admitted, she was on the verge of job burnout. The daily rides back and forth on the London tube were becoming increasingly unbearable. Just being in the city with all the hustle and bustle was a constant source of frustration in Erika's world. Her children had grown up to be respectable young men and her husband's career had grown by leaps and bounds.

Niall had long sensed that his wife was not happy. "She was great at her job," he said in a *Guardian* piece. "But she was never really happy."

For Erika it was an internal anchor that carried her through her days. But those things were outweighed by the fact that, now into her 40s, she was feeling unfulfilled and unhappy. She had read up on the idea of a midlife crisis and was feeling on the verge of one. But she had no desire to have an affair or buy a fancy sports car. Her husband had remained the one true love of her life and she had no designs on testing the relationship in that way.

So her life revolved around her family. Her work had long since turned into an emotional blur. Erika would never admit as much, but there was a sense that there had to be something on the horizon to salve her frustration.

And so Erika continued to ride the tube and read about romance.

CHAPTER FOUR
TWILIGHT'S LAST GLEAMING

Midway through 2008, Erika had reached a milestone in her own emotional journey. She had completed reading her 800th romance novel. By now, romance was pretty much all she read. The countless tales of romance and fantasy that were constantly in her thoughts had stalled her pending "midlife crisis".

Her home life continued to be pleasant. But the nature of the entertainment business being what it is, Erika was suddenly experiencing a distinct lack of work; her only job during 2007 had been a very short, one-episode stint on the *Armstrong and Miller Show*.

Late in 2008, and more to relieve boredom than anything else, Erika took in a movie, the first in the series of *Twilight* films based on the books by Stephenie Meyer. She found the horror/vampire elements to the film amusing but saw a very real love story through those trappings.

"That's what drew me in," she told miami.com.

Erika was so smitten with the notion of *Twilight* that, not long after seeing the film, she suggested to her husband that she might like to read the books. Niall took the hint and, on Christmas 2008, he presented his wife with all three of the *Twilight* books.

"Just after Christmas, I sat down and read the books and escaped for five days," she told *The Chicago Tribune*. "I just loved them. It was such a fabulous love story."

When the family went on vacation in January 2009, she read them again. She would acknowledge that the books were all of her romantic fantasies rolled into one.

"Everyone just left me alone and I went into this alternative universe," she told Pop Culture Junkies. "I would go back and see the original *Twilight* movie ten more times. Each time I would take a different friend, but I don't think they got it."

She was particularly enamored of Stephenie Meyer, who she felt was very much like her in that she was happily married with children, but had come up with an idea and just went with it.

"I was totally inspired by Stephenie Meyer," she told *Access Hollywood*. "She just flipped this switch."

That switch was that Erika was suddenly inspired to write.

However, Erika would recall that there was more to writing than inspiration from *Twilight*. "When I started writing, I was really unhappy in my job," she told *Woman and Home*. "So I escaped into writing and it took me out of my world."

It was not the first time Erika had entertained the idea of writing fiction. "I had always wanted to write," she told Bona Fide Reflections, "but I could never find the time to get beyond the first chapter or so."

On January 15, 2009, Erika pulled out her laptop, got comfortable on a living room desk her husband had bought her, so as not to disturb Niall, who was writing nearby on a table in the garden, and began writing. As she explained to *Entertainment Weekly*, Meyer and *Twilight* continued to be her guiding light.

"I came up with a story and wrote it," she said. "I had read an interview with Stephenie Meyer where she said, 'You have to start at the beginning.' So that's what I did."

But rather than a simple exercise to get her feet wet, she jumped full tilt into what would become two fairly quickly written novels.

"I wrote the first, finished that one, and then started another," she told Pop Culture Junkies. "They were kind of fan fiction in nature."

Whatever her muse was, Niall was thrilled. He was delighted with Erika's upbeat mood and was ecstatic that he was now free to watch two of his favorite shows, *The Sopranos* and *The Wire*, without his wife complaining about the violence.

From the outset, Erika was, from what she has hinted at, writing totally on instinct. "I just had to do it," she told CBC radio. "I was obsessed."

And her family was quick to adjust to the idea that when Erika would go off to a quiet part of the house and stare intently at her computer screen, she was not to be bothered. It was an easy transition for Niall and the boys to make. Niall had written the template. Now the shoe was on the other foot.

The main characters and the storylines remained vague, although Erika would hint at those early attempts as being a romance and a ghost story and the backdrop to the stories would be suspenseful. Erika knew she would infuse her stories with a very adult element that she had discovered in the volumes of romance novels she had consumed. One can only guess that there were some erotic notions at play as Erika worked away—and that both novels would be sexually charged.

Erika worked on those novels through much of 2009. During much of that time she was getting to know the world of fan fiction in which stories were based on favorite existing characters and their worlds. By April 2009, Erika cautiously decided to have some fun in this brave new world and began writing a *Twilight*-style bit of fan fiction that would feature the characters of Edward and Bella in a more mature and sexually charged universe.

"I thought I'll have a go at this," she told *Woman and Home*.

"I had read some racy bondage and submission novels," she explained during an interview on her first book tour. "I came up with the idea of what would you do if you met somebody who was into that sort of thing and you were not?"

The summary of Erika's *Twilight*-inspired fan fiction, as displayed on the fan fiction website, once read: "Bella Swan is drafted to interview a reclusive, enigmatic CEO, Edward Cullen. It is an encounter that will change her life irrevocably, leading her to the dark realms of desire."

Erika worked on her story every spare moment. Niall knew she was writing something but didn't ask her the details. Which was just as well because the idea of writing a story that included many adult sexual situations made Erika equal parts excited and embarrassed. So much so that she decided that if her manuscript ever did see the light of day, it would never go out under her real name.

What started out as a relatively simple notion quickly became a major undertaking. Over the course of three months, Erika produced a massive 1,200-page opus that took the characters of Edward and Bella into totally new territory.

"I finished it in April and then I started another one," she explained to *The Chicago Tribune*. "I kind of came to a halt in August when the manuscript [was] at 96,000 words."

Satisfied with the way the manuscript was coming together, Erika now began thinking about what she should do with her magnum opus. The initial interest in fan fiction that had led to her writing the story seemed the perfect entry into this genre and its primary domain seemed to logically be fanfiction.net.

Fanfiction.net had long been the vast repository for writers wanting to take their fictionalized adventures of their favorite stories and characters to a decidedly fan-friendly community. The efforts of those appearing on the website were considered amateur to the publishing industry and reading public at large and were often perceived as skirting the issue of copyright.

But it seemed like a safe haven for Erika to explore. To test the water, Erika knocked out an initial story in three weeks and even though she wanted to know what others thought of her writing, she decided that her work would go out under a nom de plume. She chose the very Internet-appropriate secret identity IceQueen Snowdragon. When her initial story appeared on fanfiction.net to positive response, Erika felt brave enough to begin parceling out chapters of her massive book under the title *Master of The Universe.*

Tish Beaty, a budding writer and editor, had only been reading fan fiction for a few months when she stumbled upon *Master of The Universe* in its earliest, *Twilight*-inspired incarnation and had a front-row seat as Erika's maiden effort instantly caught on with the fan fiction community. And Tish told this author there was good reason for that.

"It was a story I really liked," she recalled. "I liked the characters. I liked the storyline. I liked the whole dominant/submissive thing."

Tish, who would later go on to have a working relationship with Erika, also appreciated Erika's writing skills. "You could tell she could tell a good tale. She had a very simplistic way of writing. It was an easy read. It was all pretty straight-forward."

Even by the up and down standards of fan fiction, Erika's first story immediately jumped out. There was a maturity and energy to the work. Erika's mother, Alexandra, insisted in an Entertainmentwise story that a lot of her daughter's creative inspiration came from her Chilean/Latin roots.

Tish would acknowledge that, at the time, Erika and a handful of other fan fiction writers were "raising the bar" in terms of what had come to be expected in the fan fiction community.

Master of The Universe began appearing in episodic segments midway through the summer of 2009. And the response was immediate. The fan fiction community voraciously followed the unfolding story. *Twilight* fans were particularly vocal in their opinions of this more adult version of their beloved story. A percentage were shocked at the adult nature of the story. But many more seemed supportive of this more adult turn on their favorite characters and applauded the effort.

Tish defended Erika's take on the *Twilight* universe in a 2012 conversation with the author. "I never looked at it in terms of twisting the whole *Twilight* thing. Yes, her characters have similar attributes to the *Twilight* characters but Erika's stories are completely different."

Over the life of *Master of The Universe* on fanfiction.net, Erika's stories received an estimated 60,000 comments on various fan fiction websites. Needless to say, Erika was amazed at the response.

"I have done this as sort of an exercise to see if I could," she said in a quote that appeared in Crushable, "and I think I've proven that I can."

Toward the end of 2009, Erika was plying her trade at her day job at the BBC, this time handling the books and logistics for a series called *Naked*. Admittedly, it was difficult to keep her mind on her office work. She continued to write in her free time, fine-tuning her pre-*Masters* exercise novels that, as before, went straight from her computer to a file cabinet she had mentally labeled Limbo. But she always seemed to return to the fan fiction sites to see what was going on with *Master of The Universe*. Thoughts of a second *Master of The Universe* novel were already coursing through her head.

Because what was going on with the original was nothing short of miraculous.

Her take on Edward and Bella had become the most popular and talked about story on fanfiction.net.

Her alter ego had become the fan fiction queen of the roost. And her alter ego would routinely respond to comments, answer questions and basically bask in the community that was the tight-knit group of fan fiction readers and writers. There were invites to fan fiction conventions. Erika quite enjoyed the attention. But there were other elements of her creation to consider.

At its best, fan fiction was a very limiting proposition. It stroked the ego and sense of accomplishment. But at the end of the day, there would be little recognition in the much grander scheme of things for Erika.

And then there was the question of how much was too much.

You could only do so much with a *Twilight* story in regards to how explicit it could be and Erika sensed that she had already pushed the envelope pretty far. There had not been a hint of censorship on the part of the website but there were always those readers who felt that, even in its current form, Erika's stories were very much on the blue side.

Tish acknowledged the blowback Erika began to receive from the more puritan faction of fanfiction.net. "When it came to fanfiction.net, NC-17 was a no-no. You could have mature content but not explicit content. They do not like explicit or graphic detail on the site. From what I could see, it was turning into a problem for a lot of writers, including Erika."

And it was primarily because of the restrictions of mature and graphic elements that Erika decided that she was ready to take her story to the next step. She was once again writing and rewriting. She had always maintained that there was enough to turn the re-imagined adventures of Edward and Bella into a trilogy of novels. And a very adult trilogy that truly reflected the bold nature of what she had been reading.

It was time for Edward and Bella to become Christian and Anastasia.

CHAPTER FIVE
CAN WE TRY THIS?

The dedication page of *Fifty Shades of Grey* reads, "To Niall: The Master of My Universe." No, Erika's husband is not the inspiration for kinky stud Christian Grey. But the man who Erika had constantly praised "as a wonderful man" was very instrumental in the fashioning of his wife's very erotic odyssey.

Once Erika embarked on the reinvention of her *Twilight* story as very adult mainstream fiction, there was still the question as to what degree her project would remain under wraps. She could not tell her co-workers. The BBC had the reputation of a staid, conservative company. She was not ready to risk their reaction to her "naughty bit of business." Her children and parents? Erika was sure they would be mortified.

That left only Niall.

Erika has acknowledged that her patient and quite understanding husband was totally supportive from the *Twilight* fan fiction through the rewrites that brought Erika's creation into publication. There were some obvious lifestyle changes that had to be addressed. Erika had always worked full-time away from the house while Niall had worked primarily at home. Now they would both be working at home, albeit in different areas of the house, Erika inside and Niall primarily outside in the garden. And saint that he was, Niall willingly took over all the cooking for the family during Erika's writing process.

He was the one she turned to for editing and any continuity suggestions. And she often has recalled fondly that he did not blink an eye when he realized what kind of book his wife was writing.

She was turning out a chapter a week, which Niall would dutifully edit for grammar and punctuation. With one heated exception, when an editing argument resulted in Niall storming out of the room, their creative give and take went smoothly.

But then there were those sex scenes. Quite good and extremely hot for a first-time erotic writer.

Erika has often remarked that, like any diligent researcher, she made considerable use of the Internet, especially those websites that dealt with bondage and sadomasochism issues. She also bookmarked websites addressing the toys of the superrich; things like Gulfstream Jets, expensive Audi automobiles and Cartier watches. She viewed many porn videos, often uncomfortably so. Erika would joke at a book signing event covered by *The New York Observer* that, "If my computer was ever confiscated, social services would come and take my children away."

Erika was not merely content to gather her information from afar. In her travels she would run across members of what she often referred to as the "kinky community" and would engage them in research about how members of their lifestyle might or might not act.

"I talked to a couple of people who were into S&M," she explained to *Hollywood Life*. "I also talked to a guy online who was a submissive."

Erika had indicated that talking to members of the "kinky community" was an up and down emotional ride. Some of the people she contacted for her research made her uneasy and were not necessarily the type of people she would have chosen to be with socially. But she also made the point that she remained tolerant and, for her purposes, curious.

Then there was the question of Dr. Flynn, a pivotal character in the *Fifty Shades* storyline. Erika was light years away from being well-versed in the area of psychiatry. But she knew where to go for help.

"I talked to a child psychologist friend of mine," she told the Pattinson Post, "and then read all kinds of articles about the various issues that Christian suffers from."

Erika's research inevitably led her to the fact that contracts were often a necessity in the bottom line of a BDSM relationship. "In the stories I read that involved BDSM relationships, they never showed the paperwork," she said in an Awesomeness interview. "I was always a paperwork sort of person, so I knew that whatever I ended up writing, I would do a contract."

When she needed information on how Christian would present the pivotal contract, she discreetly consulted the legal paperwork at the BBC for a template that a sex contract might entail. She then went to a lawyer friend who guided her through the details of a finished contract that would work within the context of the story and characters.

"When she finished helping me," Erika told

miami.com, "she said, 'We will never speak of this again.'"

Erika's persistence in getting to the reality behind her fantasy was challenged when the intricacies of having sex in the backseat of an Audi R8 had to be explained in a way that would sound believable. Erika went so far as to call up the West London branch of the company that produced the vehicle in question and asked, in what she recalled in a rather sheepish blog post on Bona Fide Reflections, how a couple desiring to have sex in the backseat of their car would position themselves for a good sexual ride rather than sprained and dislocated body parts. "I rang up a local Audi salesman, told him I was writing an erotic novel and asked him if it was possible to have sex in the backseat of an Audi R8. I could hear his gasp of surprise when I asked him. He stuttered for a moment."

Once he recovered his composure, the Audi salesman insisted that such a feat was not possible in their car, primarily because the car was too small.

"I thanked him for his time and hung up. I was deeply disappointed that I could not write the scene. But it really bugged me. I thought I had to find out for myself."

And so a few days later, Erika summoned up her courage and resolve and went down to the West London headquarters of Audi. "As soon as I walked in the front door, the first car I saw was the Audi R8. I walked around the car for a minute and then plucked up the courage to go to the lady at the reception area and ask if I could get inside. She said no problem." Erika made her way back to the car. She stepped inside the backseat. She was immediately struck by the interior design, the dashboard and, most importantly for her purposes, the backseat floor.

"Oh boy! That car was sexy! I wanted to steal that car! I sat in the backseat for a bit and thought and thought. As I sat there, I thought, 'A person could totally have sex in this car.'"

She thanked the woman at the reception desk and walked out. She had no intention of buying the car. But she had what she came for.

"It was definitely a sturdy exercise," she jokingly recalled in a story that appeared on the Hollywood Life website.

All of which leads the trail back to Erika's understanding husband who was more than willing to help out with any on-the-job research. Erika has often couched answers to her sex scene research in a joking demeanor. But she has made it plain at numerous interviews and book tour Q&As that her husband's contributions did not stop at editing.

"My husband was very cooperative," she joked during an interview with *People*. "He still rolls his eyes and says, 'God! What do we have to do now?'"

Erika would go on to become more at ease in the public eye and so would occasionally drop further hints about her love life taking different directions during the writing of *Fifty Shades*. "Writing this book has definitely had its beneficial side," she joked to a boston.com reporter. "I'd say to my husband, 'I kind of need to try this' and he would say, 'Whatever you need to do.' We definitely had some fun."

However, during a book tour stop in Long Island, N.Y., in 2012, she literally brought a ballroom full of women to fits of laughter when she revealed that only some of the "research" she did with her husband actually made it to the books.

A distinctive element of writing the *Fifty Shades* books was that Erika spent quite a bit of time in setting the stage and describing in detail the interiors where scenes played out, a process she laughingly described in an interview with *UT San Diego*.

"It comes naturally," she explained. "I have to see it to write it. I need choreography and geography. I need to know how people move from one place to another. I would be writing and pulling my husband around the room to help me figure out how the characters would move. It was just so I could get things in my head. And oh yes, we were fully clothed."

But while reportedly a very willing good sport, Erika has revealed that her husband eventually got tired of all the experimentation.

Never one to be subtle, Erika related that she would often get caught up in the sexual antics of her creation. "Especially when I would reach the editing stage," she told a *Hartford Courant* reporter. "I did find myself getting quite horny."

And Erika has confirmed that much of the sex scene writing was fueled by a glass or two of wine.

For his part, Niall has been a perfect gentleman when he's been asked about his wife's work and his contribution. He's said very little.

"What is it like being married to an author of erotic fiction?" he told *The Telegraph*. "Mostly it's just like being married."

Erika spent every waking moment working on the now very adult version of her *Twilight* fan fiction. She was back at work during this period and recalled, in a

Shoreline Times interview, "I was doing a lot of writing on the train."

When inspiration struck and she was not in front of her computer, she would copy notes onto her phone and transfer them to her computer when she returned home.

"Wherever I got my inspiration, I wrote," she related in a Life Between Pages interview. "I was carrying a notebook but sometimes I would just jot something down on the back of an envelope."

However, there would be any number of places where inspiration would strike during the writing of *Fifty Shades*. An inveterate daydreamer, who admitted in a conversation with Book That Thing that "she could drift off at any moment," Erika was finding inspiration while driving her car, taking a shower and taking a cigarette break in her garden.

She has acknowledged that she had no real guidelines except for the parameters she had outlined in her *Twilight* fan fiction. It was very much an organic exercise. Erika would write and follow whichever way the writing took her. But, as she explained in an interview with the Pattinson Post, writing *Fifty Shades* was very much a routine.

"I would sit at my desk, write a paragraph and then tweet. Write another paragraph and then tweet again, etc., etc. If I wasn't in the mood to write, I would not push it. But if I was struggling I would always listen to music. For some reason, my get on and write it song was John Martyn's 'Man At The Station.' My iTunes told me that I had listened to that song 4,531 times."

But while the writing of *Fifty Shades* had turned

into a fly-by-the-seat-of-your-pants exercise, Erika admitted in an interview with website journalist Regan Walsh (aka Susan Griscom) that there were actually some parameters in place.

"I wanted to write a love story about unconditional love and how important it is," she said. "That's what I love to read and what's love without some sex thrown in?"

And when it came to writing the sex scenes, the author laughingly told *20/20* that putting enough literary drive into those scenes was a true test of her skills. "There are a lot of ways to describe an orgasm. But at a certain point I ran out of ways."

Early on, Erika was convinced that to effectively play on the mystery of Christian, she would write the story first person from Anastasia's point of view. She would also tell Walsh that laziness also had a lot to do with the choice.

"I think first person point of view is much easier to write than third person point of view. So naturally I took the easy way out."

Typically she would be found at her makeshift office in the living room with her desk facing a wall, hunched over her computer while "Man At The Station" and her other favorite music played in the headphones on her head. The music shut out most of the outside world but was also instrumental in getting her creative juices going.

When she was stuck as how to approach a specific passage, she might turn to "Toxic" by Britney Spears to coax a proper tone. When bringing Anastasia's emotions to the fore, "I'm On Fire" by Bruce Springsteen was often the catalyst. Other moments would inevitably bring the likes of Kings Of Leon, Snow Patrol and Frank Sinatra into creative play. Whether by design or subconsciously, Erika was crafting literal soundtracks to the stories in her head.

But she would inevitably find those moments when even a good song could not remove the fact that her two sons were always around and often underfoot.

"Every so often they would pop up behind me while I was typing and I did not know that they were there," she told *The Hartford Courant*. "When I would realize it, I would shut down the screen so they could not see."

But as she laughingly acknowledged during a Q&A session in London, there was a time when her children did see a bit too much of what she was doing. "One of my sons did catch me writing one day and caught the words 'nipple clamp.' He kept repeating the words over and over. It was hilarious."

Erika had long ago decided that the beginning location of *Fifty Shades* would be Seattle, Washington. It was not, as many speculated, as an homage to the *Twilight* stories, which were set in the Pacific Northwest, but rather the location of one of her guilty pleasure romance novels, *Love Song For A Raven* by Elizabeth Lowell. And, as she offered in a *Guardian* interview, the simple matter of naming a city was part and parcel of the grand adventure.

"America is much bigger and I needed a sense of distance for the story," she said. "But it was also different and exotic for me because I had never been there before. Google Street View was my friend."

Rather than simply tossing off the city of Seattle to anchor the tale and nothing more would have been the easy way out for Erika. But ever the diligent researcher, she made a detailed search of most of the Pacific Northwest, familiarizing herself with Portland, Oregon, Seattle and the Vancouver, Washington university area.

Erika brought her own experiences as a student at the University of Kent into play when it came to fleshing out Anastasia's background as a college student.

And by the time she had settled on the Pacific Northwest for her setting, it had become a foregone conclusion that the characters of Christian and Anastasia would be American as a nod to her *Twilight* fan fiction that had started it all.

But that turn caused Erika no end of problems when it came to wrapping her writing mind around all things American. She reported on several stops on her book tour that U.S. traditions like baseball caused her no end of headaches, as witnessed by the time she described a home run as fourth base.

At this point in the writing process, Erika's foray into adult fiction was still largely a hybrid. Although the names of the main characters had been changed to Christian and Anastasia to reflect the more explicit/erotic nature of the work, there was still much in the story that continued to reflect the *Twilight*/fan fiction feel of the first incarnation.

But Erika was well aware that while *Twilight* had served her well in the first incarnation of the tale, as clean a break as possible from that realm was necessary. She was self-editing as she went along; eliminating or altering what she felt were particular elements of that world and replacing them with actions and emotions that would seem more appropriate in a more sophisticated and much more adult world. There was an instinctive sense in Erika that she knew she had to tread lightly so as to not dilute her story.

"While I was writing, I basically gave the characters their head," she explained in a Bookish Temptations interview. "They went in a completely different direction than I had originally intended. There was one scene in *Fifty Shades of Grey* that I had to write three times in order to make it work. It was the scene after the dinner party at Christian's parents' house where Anastasia is leaving Christian. The way it finally worked out was that Christian spanks her. But it did not start out that way."

With all the improvisation, starts and stops inherent in her writing process, Erika watched in amazement as the stack of manuscript pages grew. She told Regan Walsh the length had not been by design. "I didn't plan on writing quite so much. But Christian and Anastasia felt so passionately about each other, that's just the way the story went."

One of the more endearing surprises was the day Erika introduced the tagline "Laters Babe" to the world. Anyone looking for a stroke of divine inspiration for the line would be disappointed as Erika reported that an older nephew quite simply said "laters" to her one day and the idea just grew from there.

Erika's confidence level rose as the story continued to unfold. While still occasionally reticent to tell those in her family what she was up to, Erika told My Secret Romance that by the time her more adult work began to unfold, it was public knowledge in her workplace at the BBC.

"Once I started writing, I had no problem telling people at work what I did. I think you get to a certain age and you really don't give a toss what people think. I am constantly being teased by my colleagues. But at this point, I just kind of brazen it out."

Erika worked diligently through the remaining months of 2009. And she had no illusions about the quality of her writing. She laughed at the notion that her effort might be Pulitzer Prize quality in an interview with *Today*.

"I'm not a very disciplined writer," she said. "It's very raw. There is nothing revolutionary about the prose, the plot or the characters."

But she would acknowledge at a book tour event that, by the time she was nearing the end of the third book, she was determined that she had done the right thing by her story and herself.

"I wrote the book for myself," she told a rapt audience. "You need to write about your passion and what you like. At the end of the day, it's about what you want to do."

Much had been made about Erika's level of writing talent. But the reality was that, in all fairness, while never approaching the level of perceived talent many attached to their greatest authors, she had quite naturally evolved into a quite competent writer.

Fifty Shades of Grey was a raw first element, replete with clichés, redundancies and pedestrian plot turns. The first book was still anchored, to a large extent, by its *Twilight* roots and fairly predictable characterization. But shining through was the fact that *Fifty Shades of Grey* would be eminently readable, a classic page-turner.

By the time Erika arrived at *Fifty Shades Darker*, she was definitely a work in progress. Many of the technical abrasions of the first book had been rounded off and smoothed out. Deep and detailed characterization had grown into a legitimate element of the storyline. And it was obvious to readers that Erika had grown in confidence to the point where she would brave some dark corners that added needed substance to this kinky love story.

Fifty Shades Freed was most certainly the most challenging volume of the trilogy. The characters were moving in some complicated arcs and Erika was faced with the daunting task of wrapping it all up in a conclusion that would satisfy herself and her fans. Her prose remained largely raw and to the point at the end, and, while there was still a sense of awkwardness about it all, the *Fifty Shades* series would be looked at as a final literary path successfully negotiated.

As she neared the end of the third and final element of the *Fifty Shades* trilogy, she was seemingly at a loss as to what to do next. Taking this version of her work back to fanfiction.net did not seem to make sense. And part of her had to acknowledge that there might ultimately be some financial gain in what she had done.

James had indicated on several occasions that, early on, she did make some queries to large mainstream publishers but received little interest in her manuscript.

With that initial round of rejections, she remained cautious on the subject of turning to professional publishing. Choosing instead to create her own website, fifty shades.com, she released her reworked erotic saga under her control. By late 2009, her website was up and ready to go. Her insecurity and unease at venturing into this uncharted territory would be reflected in the fact that the earliest chapters up on her Fifty Shades site would feature a banner with the *Master of The Universe* title. But Erika must have known in her heart that the reworking was taking her into uncharted territory and that she could no longer even think of calling the book *Master of The Universe*. And so she cast about for a more appropriate title. According to an interview with Bookish Temptations, the search did not take very long.

"I liked the phrase Fifty Shades. It fit in with the idea of who this enigmatic man was. So I stuck with that."

The only thing remaining was an author's name.

Still leery of the impact her writing could have on her professional life and the private lives of her family, Erika decided on yet another pseudonym.

"I thought I would continue working and writing on the side," she told a London audience. "So I thought I'd have two identities and then I would be able to do that. If I had realized that I was going to be such a best-seller, I probably would have used my own name. But actually, I think that having this other identity is really kind of cool."

So Erika sat down and wondered what her name should be. There has been some speculation that she turned to the names of her favorite romance authors for inspiration. But the reality was that this major decision did not require much thought at all.

"To be honest, I really didn't give it a huge amount of thought," she admitted to boston.com. "In three minutes, I thought of E L James. James is kind of a family name. E is for Erika.

"I'm not going to tell you what the L stands for."

But what she would admit to was an extreme case of fatigue connected to the writing of the books. In a sense, she was saying goodbye to *Fifty Shades* as she told a London fan get together.

"It was a bloody relief. The last thing I wrote when I wrote the epilogue was, 'Thank you for supporting me. This has been a blast and will the last person here please turn off the lights.' That's how I felt. It was very emotional."

And even with the first brush of success and what would soon be the tidal wave of more *Fifty Shades*, James recalled in a 2012 fan get together that, when she had finished *Fifty Shades Freed*, that was literally the end for her.

"If there's no conflict, there's no story. If I ever want to continue on, then it's like 'what the fuck can I do?' I mean I've thrown the kitchen sink at them (the books)."

CHAPTER SIX
DOWN UNDER

Amanda Hayward was on a voyage of self-discovery not unlike that of E L James. And not unlike the London-based author, the New South Wales, Australia wife and mother had settled into a happy but predictable existence.

"I was bored," she explained to *The Sydney Morning Herald*. "I was doing nothing other than looking after the kids."

One day, while searching for something to read, she stumbled upon a website for fan fiction. Amanda was drawn to the idea of amateurs writing new stories based on their favorite characters and books and, with the encouragement of her husband, she began to peruse this brave new world.

At the time, fan fiction was considered a backwater community, a loose amalgamation of people enamored of a series of books or television characters who wanted to express their devotion by creating original stories. Some say the conceit started with *Star Trek* and has, most recently, been carried on with *Twilight*. But the bottom line was that people who lived and breathed a favorite, but did not have the inclination to attempt to write original material on a professional level, now had an outlet for it.

Amanda had not been on long when she came across *Master of The Universe*. She was impressed with the bravery of it all and the ease in which Leonard put her story and characters through their creative paces. She continued to follow Erika's creation and found a real break in her daily routine in the regular installments.

Amanda would find many kindred spirits in cyberspace; one of those was Jenny Pedroza, a third-grade teacher and mother from Arlington, Texas. The pair hit it off immediately and would be in constant contact, expressing their thoughts and creative notions.

In a similar manner, Amanda and Tish Beaty had become Internet pals around January 2010, with their conversations inevitably turning to the current state of publishing. Tish recalled that the conversation of their own possible venture often entered the conversation.

"She said that she was really interested in starting a publishing house as a branch site to the existing Writer's Coffee Shop site. I thought it was an excellent idea and we started working together."

For her part, Amanda was driven by her unwavering belief that much of fan fiction was as good as, if not superior, to what was being published by the major publishers.

"The more I got involved with it," Hayward explained on a story that appeared on The Writer's Coffee Shop website, "the more I discovered so many stories from authors. There were so many creative people that needed a publisher with the guts to put their work out there."

Amanda's enthusiasm grew as her involvement in the fan fiction world grew. In September 2009, she took things a step forward when she launched an informal discussion website with the working title of The Writer's Coffee Shop.

Into 2010, Erika was beginning to reap a semblance of notoriety for *Master of The Universe*. She was invited to several fan fiction get togethers. One particular highlight was an appearance on a panel discussing fan fiction at the famed San Diego Comic Con. "I loved the craziness of Comic Con," she gushed to *UT San Diego*. "It was surreal and a lot of fun."

In the meantime, Amanda continued to grow in the fan fiction community. January 26, 2010 saw the launch of The Library, a free website in which people were free to post links of their own fan fiction for people to read.

Among those who responded to The Library was E L James with her newly christened adult version of *Master of The Universe*. Amanda was immediately impressed with the maturity and, yes, the adult nature of this reimagining. She saw a lot of potential in Erika's work.

Potential that went light years beyond the fan fiction world.

Erika was heartened to find that her adult version of her *Twilight* fan fiction was once again a much-talked about center of many readers' worlds. And the responses ran the gamut. Some loved it. Some disliked it to varying degrees but continued to ask for more chapters. Erika remained happily surprised at the reactions. She remained shy at the notion of a 40-something mother from suburbia penning such heated erotica. With the exception of her husband, few of Erika's friends and acquaintances knew her secret and the ones she did confide in, she made them promise not to tell a soul.

Amanda Hayward was one of countless readers who lived and died by Erika's erotic adventure. But beyond the pure enjoyment of escaping into Erika's world, Amanda's interest went a bit further. Through her website The Library, Amanda found herself in communication and reading a number of authors. Encouraged by the prospect of so much talent going unnoticed, she, along with partners Jenny Pedroza, Tish Beaty and Jennifer McGuire, launched The Writer's Coffee Shop as a full-blown e-book publisher in October 2010.

Tish was instantly on-board as both the Acquisitions Managing Editor and editor. In that capacity she brought author Miya Kressin and *The Hunter And The Hunted* book out of fan fiction and into the publishing light. Within the first six months The Writer's Coffee Shop was off and running as a legitimate e-book publisher. Albeit one that was operating on a shoestring.

"I wasn't getting paid for the initial work that I did," disclosed Tish. "Amanda and I had an understanding that, once I began editing, I would be getting more. Originally she talked about bringing me in as a 20 percent partner. But the reality was that, at the time, there was not a lot of money coming in and the agreement was that once the money started coming in, I would get paid."

Amanda was attempting something that was very much in its infancy. There had been few who had taken the e-book publishing plunge at that point and then with only marginal success. The Writer's Coffee Shop would be flying in the face of a whole lot of unwritten publishing laws.

It was the very rare manuscript that came in over the transom and was plucked out of the slush pile. Agents were considered the keys to the mainstream publishing kingdom. But, with the economy in the tank and bookstores closing right and left, publishers were being very selective and going with sure things and brand names rather than, again with rare exceptions, taking a chance on a talented unknown.

With e-book publishing and the print on-demand coming into its own, Amanda felt her concept would be cost-effective enough for her to pick up worthy talents and get them into the book-buying market place.

For her part, Erika was largely naive about e-book publishing. What she did know was limited to the amateur fan fiction community. What she was doing was a lot of fun to do and it was good for her ego. But only in her wildest fantasies did she ever consider a viable publishing outlet that would break her out into a universe of readers and, hope against hope, make some money from her efforts. She sensed that those opportunities were out there but did not have a clue of how to reach them.

Tish recalled that Amanda and she had heard through the grapevine that Erika was "shopping around and possibly looking to publish." "Amanda and I had talked about it and thought it would be a good thing for the publishing house."

As these things often transpire, everybody's take on the true chronology seemed to differ.

Amanda had related that even before the official launch of The Writer's Coffee Shop, she had already had Erika on her radar, emailing and texting the author and making a big push to sign with her company and publish her stories online.

"When we started to look at the possibility of starting The Writer's Coffee Shop, we knew E L James' story would make a great addition to our titles," Pedroza told the author in a 2012 email Q&A.

Already leery of the notoriety her story was beginning to generate and a bit unsure with the idea of her real name coming out, Erika was flattered but not ready to take that leap. But Amanda was nothing if not persistent.

"Amanda worked for ten months to get her signed," Pedroza told *The Star Telegram*. "She was very shy."

Amanda echoed those sentiments in a CNN World feature. "She was very reserved and was very unsure and didn't think there would be a market for it (her book)."

Tish echoed the notion that Erika was a bit shy about taking that next step. "She wasn't ready at the time. I'm not really sure why. I just know that, at the time, she was not comfortable enough to publish. She was not ready to take that next step."

In a later interview with the author, Pedroza would acknowledge that Amanda and Erika had become good friends but that did not necessarily make negotiations any easier. "Amanda spent many months in discussion with Ms. James."

Tish agreed with the notion that the courtship had gone on several months but admitted to being unsure to what degree Amanda may or may not have been contacting Erika. "I was under the impression that we were leaving her alone and not bothering her."

But, as the discussions played out, Erika proved to be very business-like and practical in guiding the fortunes of her story. "I know that she wanted to see how we did," related Tish. "She knew that we were a new publishing house and she wanted to see how we worked and how the books were published and sold. She was totally business. She was doing her homework. She did not want to jump in right off, which is understandable."

Once her own Fifty Shades website was up and running, she immediately removed her previous work from fanfiction.net and directed her already substantial audience to her new website for a different take on her previous tale. There was some grumbling from hardcore fan fiction readers that Erika was looking to make some money off the goodwill she had generated in the fan fiction community. And once the first chapters of the "more adult" *Master of The Universe* began to appear, the first questions regarding copyright infringement (an ongoing grey area in the fan fiction world) were heard.

But Erika was too preoccupied with other things to consider those charges. There was her husband and children to consider and, amid the growing intrusion of her writing, she was stalwart in maintaining a sense of normalcy around the house.

But, as she told *Newsday*, her boys were conspicuous by their absence from her attention. "I ignored my sons while writing the books," she said. "I'm a great believer in benign neglect. But they're boys and at this age they don't have much to say anyway."

Work at the BBC continued to be sporadic but there was now talk of an upcoming television pilot that would most certainly require her expertise.

Amid all this was the regular correspondence from Amanda, extolling the virtues of e-book publishing and that a successful book, most certainly hers, could be lucrative. "Every month or so, Amanda would contact me and hassle me," she chuckled during a My Secret Romance interview.

Erika was wavering. She discussed the proposal from Amanda with Niall who, with his professional experience in the writing trade, was the perfect sounding board. He knew what questions to ask and where to check the fine print. And he did agree that a successful book would, indeed, make money.

At one point, Erika related to Fiction Vixen, she actually went to Amanda and said yes to her offer to publish. "But then I got cold feet. They persisted. Then I realized that, if I did not agree to publish, somebody else would have and it would have been without my permission and that would have broken my heart. So finally I said yes."

Tish did not necessarily believe that there was one thing that ultimately tipped her in the direction of signing with The Writer's Coffee Shop. "I think she just kind of got all her ducks in a row and was ready. It just took some time for her to be ready."

Fear of having her work somehow stolen was only part of the reason Erika agreed to sign with the Australian publisher. Insecurity was the other, as she explained in *Publishers Weekly*. "I didn't try any larger, more conventional forms of publishing, preferring to dip my toe first into the publishing world with a small, very supportive publishing house."

By New Year's Eve 2010, Erika had made her decision. In January 2011, she signed on the dotted line with The Writer's Coffee Shop. "We were all thrilled when Ms. James made the decision to sign with us," recalled Pedroza.

But even on the relatively small scale that The Writer's Coffee Shop operated on, not everybody at the company was completely sold on the James signing.

Donna Huber, the head of marketing for the Australian company, reflected on her feelings of the signing in a blog post on Bona Fide Reflections.

"I remember the night that our publisher, Amanda Hayward, told me that we had signed E L James and her *Fifty Shades* trilogy. While Amanda was excited, I was filled with a bit of trepidation. I knew of E L James from the online writing community and had even checked out her story. My first thought was that, I'm going to have to promote erotica and do so without blushing."

Huber had been around the publishing industry long enough to know the realities. And the fact that James' books would be such a gamble concerned her. "I knew E L had a large following online but there was no guarantee that it would follow her into the publishing realm. And there was the root of my trepidation. Would I be working with an author who expected to be on *The New York Times* best-seller list right out of the gate?"

After the contracts were signed, there were some

realities to deal with before the first volume in the trilogy would come out to everybody's satisfaction. And that was to make sure that Erika's work was now washed of any and all *Twilight* references.

Tish recalled that Amanda had chosen her to edit the first volume of the *Fifty Shades* trilogy because "she felt I was the only one in the publishing house who they trusted with Erika's book." Amanda also indicated to her editor that *Fifty Shades of Grey* would require a delicate hand. This would not be a heavy red pen marking kind of editing job. Tish, who by her own estimation had been "hard on writers in the editing phase," was instructed to go easy.

Shortly after a deal was struck, Tish did an initial read-through of *Fifty Shades of Grey*. The editor admitted that her work with The Writer's Coffee Shop had kept her busy and that she had not seen the later installments of *Master of The Universe* or the version of the story that Erika had posted on her own Fifty Shades site. But she was now encouraged by what she had read.

"At that point, I think she had done a really good job of making the story her own. She had stuck with the original story that all her fans had loved. The basics were still there. She had used Stephenie Meyer's characters to inspire her story but it was still her story. At that point it was not *Twilight*."

Erika had already done a very good job in editing her manuscript and it went without saying that the sex scenes, as they now read, were nowhere to be found in her fan fiction version of her story.

Before she got down to the business of editing *Fifty Shades of Grey*, Tish recalled her introductory conversation with Erika as being cordial and to the point.

"I introduced myself to her and basically told her how I worked," she said. "I told her the things I looked for and, if she had any questions about the suggestions I was making, to let me know."

The editor found Erika to be laid-back yet very business-like. They were on good terms after their initial discussion but Tish came away knowing full well that Erika knew exactly what she wanted and was not about to compromise her creative principles.

"Initially we were just going to be looking at the content," the editor recalled of the plan of action regarding editing. "Erika had already made a lot of changes in the content and those were things she really wanted me to look for. She wanted to make sure it all meshed together."

The time frame for editing *Fifty Shades of Grey* was pegged at six weeks. The editing process began late in March. By that time, Tish already had a mental list of what issues would need to be addressed.

"The big thing was that there would be flow within the story in terms of turning a story that was coming from fan fiction to a finished published book. Structure, grammar, things like that; making the changes that needed to be made and for the story to make sense."

The editor knew going in that certain things would be off-limits to her. She would not be looking for character issues which, in Erika's vision, were set in stone. Nor could she touch the sex scenes. "It was her story. I wasn't there to change it."

Tish recalled that one day, during a rather heated

discussion, she inadvertently said something that was taken as an insult by Erika. The editor did not remember what the particulars of the insult were but she did recall that she immediately apologized and that everything was fine after that.

"I think that we got along fairly well. She's a witty person but it was obvious throughout the process that her work was her work. If there was something I suggested or did that she wasn't happy with, then we would talk it out and compromise. It can be kind of hard when you have an author from the U.K. and an editor from the States. It was kind of a tricky process but I think that we got through it just fine."

With the initial editing done to everybody's satisfaction, one final hurdle remained: a seven-hour, three-way Skype hook-up between Erika, Tish and a beta reader based in Australia. This page-by-page final pass before publication resulted in a few minor details being dealt with and then the process was over.

"I felt pretty good about the way things had gone. There were some things that I would have liked to change. But it was her story. It wasn't my job to make those changes. So sure, I thought I did a real good job for Erika."

Unfortunately, Erika did not think so.

James was candid in stating that the initial round of editing through The Writer's Coffee Shop was less than successful in a far-reaching interview catalogued by Red Carpet News.

"It was a two-fold editing process because the books were edited by someone and, unfortunately, the first person who worked on them did not know what they were doing.

"But I didn't know that at the time. The second editor was lovely. Because of the way the story was originally written, a segment at a time, there was a lot of repetition that had to be dealt with."

Tish was well aware that James had ultimately been less than thrilled with how the editing of *Fifty Shades of Grey* went. But in an interview in 2012, she refused to take the blame for what transpired.

"I did not end up editing books two and three," she candidly explained. "What happened was, after *Fifty Shades of Grey* was published, Erika got slammed pretty hard because there were some copy-editing typos in the book. A big part of the problem was that, at the time, The Writer's Coffee Shop did not have a copy editor on staff. The copy-editing typos really ticked Erika off. She was embarrassed and aggravated that her book had been published with some mistakes in it. The reason I got for not editing the next two books was that Erika had not been happy with the edits on the first book."

Well aware of James' public comments regarding her editing, Tish has continued to wish the author well and remains thrilled at her success.

"All I can say is that I did what I was asked to do by the publishing house," she declared. "I edited her the way they asked me to edit her. I could have gone in there and red-penned the manuscript really hard and made it a little bit less of a pleasant experience for everybody involved. But, at the time, that was not what was expected of me."

Following the editing controversy, Tish's responsibilities with the company were gradually diminished. By February 2012, Tish Beaty was no longer with The Writer's Coffee Shop. "I was kind of weeded out of The Writer's Coffee Shop as the *Fifty Shades* books gained in popularity. I guess you could say I was kind of the fall guy."

Pedroza, on the other hand, related to the author in the most positive way that the editing process for *Fifty Shades of Grey* was nothing if not smooth. "Ms. James' original story was loosely based on the *Twilight* books and so everybody knew that there had to be a lot of rewriting and reworking of the manuscript. Ms. James was extremely professional and worked well with our editors to help make the process work. And because the length of the original manuscript was so long, the decision was made to split the manuscript into three separate books."

Of major concern to Erika was that her books would have an appropriate but not too risqué cover. "I wanted very simple covers that I would not be embarrassed to have somebody see me reading on the tube," she told My Secret Romance. "And they all had to have some items that were in the story."

The search for the undone bowtie that graced the cover of *Fifty Shades of Grey* was a particularly arduous challenge. Erika initially wanted the bowtie to be black but could not find the appropriate image. Amanda suggested that the bowtie be silver and found the right image but not in the right format for a book cover. A designer was brought in and a cover featuring the titular neckwear was created.

"When I saw the tie in a portrait format, I know that's what I wanted," she told My Secret Romance. "The mask for the second book was much easier to find."

With the editing and cover art locked in place, Erika held her breath when The Writer's Coffee Shop announced the release date of the first of three E L James books, *Fifty Shades of Grey*. In a fantasy sort of way, not unlike her stories, she now felt she was truly E L James.

What her alter ego would bring to her life was anybody's guess.

CHAPTER SEVEN
E L LOVES CG

What's in the name Christian Grey? According to E L James, quite a bit. It was the name of the character in her first, still unpublished novel that she attempted after reading the *Twilight* books.

"I loved the name," she tweeted Tongue Twied in 2010. "I love how strong the name Christian is. And I admit that I easily likened the character of Christian Grey to the character Dr. Christian Troy from the television show *Nip/Tuck* because he was also quite confident in his sexual exploits."

And his sexuality was uppermost in James' mind when creating the character of Christian Grey, as she explained at a London interview/signing event. "Christian is definitely my fantasy figure," she chuckled. "I definitely wanted to shag him and then fix him up."

Initially, James' idea of Christian Grey seemed to be fairly straightforward. He was equal measures of the male characters from *Beauty And The Beast*, *Pretty Woman* and Mr. Rochester from *Jane Eyre*. But as the writing progressed, her creation began to fly in a myriad of directions.

From the outset, it was the exploits, attitudes and agendas of Christian Grey that drove the engine that was *Fifty Shades of Grey*. Far from a romance novel cliché and cipher, the dashing, bent and extremely flawed billionaire was also created with an extremely deep and mysterious character arc in mind.

James has acknowledged that the idea of making Christian was less a flight of fantasy than a reflection of a certain reality. She was well aware that there were people like Christian in the world and felt that building the character against a backdrop of unbridled wealth would open up the landscape of the story.

And James has readily admitted that he was a tough character to wrap her creative mind around. "Christian really is a tough headspace to be in," she explained on the website TrueTwihard4ever. "The reason I made Christian so complex and damaged was that it made for a more interesting story. If he wasn't damaged then the narrative just would not work."

James has made a point of playing up Christian Grey as her "fantasy man" and, during extensive press interviews and book tours, has played with the notion that she might have had a Christian Grey type in her past. James acknowledged the often-asked question of whether Christian Grey was indeed real on her website when she said, "Now that would be telling." And during a book tour stop in Miami she said, with tongue firmly planted in cheek, "Christian Grey is based on a real person. Last I heard he was living in South Africa."

But beyond the hype and statements intended to shock and, by association, gather tabloid headlines, it becomes obvious the more James talks about Christian Grey, the more interesting he becomes.

And she has indicated on several occasions that a large attraction to the character rests on his imperfect nature.

James saw Christian as an emotional virgin, seemingly incapable of certain human emotions and ultimately an interesting counter to Anastasia's physical virginity.

"Christian Grey is a complicated, damaged and talented man," she explained to *USA Today*. "He's very capable, strong and domineering. But he's also very broken."

She was quick to add in an ABC News interview that he is also the perfect fantasy man. "Christian is fucked up," she laughed. "But Christian is also good looking, very wealthy, knows what he's doing in bed and needs to be loved. Who wouldn't want this man?"

Especially when readers dig below the character's sadistic side and find what James said in a Daily Beast article about Christian "having a very sad side." In that same article, in which the concept of spanking in a real world was given a thorough examination, the writer points out that Christian Grey is "very solicitous and apologetic for a sadist" and, in terms of his relationship with Anastasia, is probably "the easiest difficult man of all time."

James made the point in a conversation with *People* that it is those strengths and weaknesses that have made the character so attractive to women. "His dominating nature is not necessarily what women are looking for in real life. But that quality is very attractive on paper because women want to unravel this mystery man."

Which is why James was quick to build the psychic

kink of being a full-blown dom (dominant) into his character profile in this bondage/discipline/sadism/masochism relationship.

"I was fascinated by BDSM and why anyone would want to be in this lifestyle. I think the whole idea of this lifestyle is hot as hell. How such a person acts and is in control is very appealing. Christian as a fantasy guy kind of evolved out of that notion."

At the end of the day, the question is simple. Why is Christian Grey in the hearts and libidos of so many women? James offered up a reason in a conversation with *People*.

"You're in charge of your job, your house, your children and getting food on the table. It's just nice for someone else to be in charge for a bit."

Adding to the appeal of a fantasy man to fantasy readers, she further explored the hot commodity she created in the Pattinson Post when she quipped, "We all like a man who knows what to do and Christian Grey knows what to do."

The author admitted in a *Sun* piece that she did indeed harbor some semblance of a fantasy of having a Christian Grey in her life. "Perhaps I would like to be told how to dress, eat and behave. But only for about ten minutes."

However, James quickly warned readers in a *Los Angeles Times* article that her Christian Grey is pure fantasy and that nobody should seriously hope to bump into him on the street.

"I think being with somebody like that would be hell on earth. At the end of the day, we want somebody who is going to do the bloody dishes."

And that somebody is not Christian Grey.

CHAPTER EIGHT
A DATE WITH ANASTASIA

James did not have to look very far when it came to naming her *Fifty Shades* heroine. All the inspiration she needed was in her education back pages.

"I immediately thought of the Russian family," she tweeted Tongue Twied in 2010. "I did my dissertation at university on the fall of the Tsar of Russia and since then I've always liked the name Anastasia."

On the surface, Anastasia Steele seems oh-so prototypical. She is young, innocent, extremely naive and, it goes without saying, a virgin. That she would come within blocks of a Christian Grey does not remotely ring true.

But reality has nothing to do with *Fifty Shades* and so, in the classic "good girl meets bad boy" scenario, Anastasia willingly enters into a relationship where she will be totally dominated and, dare to say, changed forever.

James explained in a London signing event that was posted by Red Carpet News that Anastasia's virginity was the most interesting element of her character in terms of building character.

"If people have been around the block a few times, they know what to expect. Let's face it, if you've done it all before, you know exactly what's going to happen. If you haven't, you don't know anything. It's a great device. People like Anastasia do exist. I was a bit like that... a long time ago."

However, Anastasia is not merely a blow-up doll in human form. She is spunky in a way, resourceful and, as the odyssey progressed, has been more than capable of giving as good as she gets.

"Anastasia knows what she wants from this relationship," James told Fiction Vixen. "When I started, I knew that she would be the stronger of the two, although, in the beginning, I did not think that was obvious. But her character and her strengths evolved that way."

Fiction Vixen was further clued in by James on how looks, when it came to Anastasia, could be deceiving.

"She's shy and subdued and so Christian thinks that she's ideal submissive material. But of course she's not and she derails him completely. Underneath all the blushing and flushing, she's incredibly strong. She won't do as she's told and that's a novelty for him."

But as we all know, *Fifty Shades* is not a woman's liberation polemic dressed up in S&M trappings. The erotic elements and Anastasia's sexual awakening are very real and, as she is schooled in Christian's particular brand of sex education, she becomes an enticing player. Let's face it, what man could resist the moments when Anastasia looks into Christian Grey's eyes and bites her lip?

James offered in an *Entertainment Weekly* interview that the gesture might well have been Anastasia's secret weapon.

"If you think about it, what's erotic about someone's mouth is their lips or biting," said James. "That's what drives men wild."

CHAPTER NINE
GONE VIRAL

Fifty Shades of Grey was scheduled to be published on May 26, 2011. James was thrilled at the prospect of her story seeing the light of day in a more professional setting. But her goals for the book remained modest

Those who James confided in regarding her literary efforts had been politely supportive and encouraging. But, as she offered in a conversation with *The Herald Sun*, they were often quick to derail her ultimate dream. "I had always wanted to be published," she said. "But everybody told me that there was no way a book like mine would be."

Expectations remained high. The Writer's Coffee Shop had a limited budget when it came to marketing its authors. It went without saying that a big-budget marketing campaign was out of the question. There would be a small print on-demand element to the release but the majority of any sales would come from e-books. And, when it came to that element of the burgeoning online book publishing industry, The Writer's Coffee Shop had definitely done its homework.

Throughout its existence, The Writer's Coffee Shop had made a point of plugging into the online fan fiction and romance and erotic romance communities. Consequently, by the time *Fifty Shades of Grey* was ready for publication, The Writer's Coffee Shop could count on an estimated 60,000 friends to, hopefully, spread the word. The fuse was in place.

It would remain for the website Goodreads to supply the match.

Goodreads.com launched its reader recommendation website in 2007 and almost immediately became a major player in the e-book publishing pipeline. Its popularity and lighthearted yet authoritative tone in recommending books has, to date, swelled its readership ranks to 9,600,000.

A more dramatic story on how the website was integral to breaking *Fifty Shades* was circulated. Reportedly Goodreads ran a review of *Fifty Shades of Grey* in June 2011. The rave review caused an immediate increase in interest and e-book sales. The groundswell of early support from Goodreads grew as Twitter gossip, chatter on celebrity websites and just plain word of mouth began to expand *Fifty Shades*' grip on public consciousness.

However, Goodreads Features Editor Jessica Donaghy set the record straight in a 2012 email response to the author. "No one review led to the popularity of *Fifty Shades*," she said. "Rather, it was the book's early readers wrote reviews on Goodreads and recommended it to their friends who, in turn, recommended the book to their friends."

Donaghy, who acknowledged that the groundswell of support did, indeed, begin in the summer of 2011, said that a big part of the early support came from a couple of factions under the Goodreads umbrella. "A couple of romance-focused reading groups, each with about 2,000-4,000 members, picked up the book as their next read and those early readers rated the book very highly. And so a best-seller was born through word of mouth."

Jenny Pedroza offered that the advances in e-book and online technology proved to be The Writer's Coffee Shop's viral ace in the hole in piling up the hits and ultimately sales for *Fifty Shades of Grey*.

"The original online story already had a very large following and Ms. James was very social and friendly with many of them. This online base had a huge impact on the marketing of the novel. Through sites like Facebook, Twitter, Goodreads and Amazon, word quickly spread. That the book was so easy to get through e-book applications only helped to boost sales."

As did the first brushes with mainstream reviews. Admittedly reviews of *Fifty Shades of Grey* were mixed but it was a major breakthrough that any reviewer outside the romance fiction realm would even bother with what they considered trifle reading. James' less-than-literary writing was an easy target for many reviewers, as was the raw spirit and tone of the book.

Entertainment Weekly gave the book a B-plus grade and praised it "for being in a class by itself." *The Guardian* stated, "It is jolly, eminently readable and is as sweet and safe as BDSM can be." And in a classic backhanded compliment, *The Columbus Dispatch* opined, "Despite the clunky prose, James does cause one to turn the page."

For her part, James, normally shy at the notion of doing press, embraced the idea of online promotion and, between June 21-June 30, engaged in a mini round of e-book promotion with what was called the *Fifty Shades of Grey* Blog Tour, in which she posted blog entries, did interviews and sponsored online promotions and giveaways.

While considered a minor promotion, marketing director Huber found that James was the ultimate good soldier when it came to promotion. "Just because it was a virtual tour did not mean that it was any less time consuming. The humor that was so prevalent in her book is also present in her daily life, which had been a big help during this crazy tour schedule for both of us. Even with the success she has had, she has been a true team player. The emails I would get from her and her very British ways would always make me smile."

The *Fifty Shades of Grey* blog tour was the ideal entry for James into the world of publicity. The questions were largely softball in nature, the interviewers were more fans than hard-bitten journalists and the sheer repetition helped her hone good responses and interview techniques that fit her personality. There was still a sense of privacy in this kind of press that James appreciated.

But while she appeared to have a good handle on the publicity nature of it all, she was still cautious and very conscious of keeping her true identity a secret. She would insist on only being referred to as E L by interviewers and those privy to her earliest interviews could sense through the stumbling and occasional stammering that she was uncomfortable in the spotlight. And that the more distance she could put between E L James and Erika Leonard the better.

But she could sense that the time would come when she would have to go public with it all.

Lyss Stern, a New York wife/mother and blogger of her very fem-friendly site Divalysscious Moms, discovered firsthand how quickly *Fifty Shades of Grey* fever had taken hold. Shortly after its publication, Stern recalled being alerted to the book by a friend in Los Angeles. She read it, was instantly hooked and, as she explained to PageDaily, so were many others in a below-the-radar, clandestine way.

"It had not yet taken off in New York," she recalled. "After I read it I knew that it was something that every woman needed to read. I began blogging about it on Facebook and on my own website Divalysscious Moms. I quickly noticed moms reading the book at playgrounds and I heard them gush over it when I dropped my boys off at school."

What Stern sensed, and rightly so, was that *Fifty Shades* was a legitimate movement in the making. It was all word of mouth and very undercover. But like all movements, she could predict that *Fifty Shades* would eventually enter mainstream consciousness.

Stern's observations were being magnified a thousand-fold. Women of all ages (making the term "Mommy Porn" a true misnomer) were taking time out of their day to read *Fifty Shades of Grey* and to lose themselves in the erotic fantasy.

The stories of where and when women were finding time to read *Fifty Shades of Grey* were becoming the new urban legends. On planes, in the office, in their cars. Impromptu book clubs and discussion groups were popping up in which women were having good laughs as well as frank discussions on the implications of the book and a new lease on their sexual lives. On one level it was becoming a bit of a hoot. But most importantly, *Fifty Shades of Grey* had suddenly become the literary gatekeeper to a whole new world. And word of mouth was singing its praises with the fervor of a gospel choir.

Looking back on the early reception to *Fifty Shades* in a *20/20* interview, James made a point that, to a large extent, the story had been overlooked in the rush to praise the frank sexuality of the tale. "A big part of the fantasy for women is the idea of being protected and spoiled by a man."

Fifty Shades of Grey played right into the hands of the burgeoning e-book technology. Those who were interested in the book but did not want to suffer the unease and possible embarrassment of buying a copy in an actual bookstore could order an e-copy online and no one would be the wiser.

They were secure and, most likely, emboldened by Internet technology as the modern equivalent of the plain brown wrapper.

Needless to say, word of mouth rather than the traditional publicity approach was turning *Fifty Shades of Grey* into a surprise underground hit along the e-book superhighway. Amanda at The Writer's Coffee Shop was happily amazed. James was simply flabbergasted by the news.

"I'm staggered by this," she told the Associated Press. "I never thought it would do this."

And because The Writer's Coffee Shop now had what would be termed their first breakout hit, the company was no doubt working hard to catch up to the realities of suddenly having a book that everybody seemed to want.

Marketing director Huber had a front-row seat to how James was reacting to the early success and offered in the Bona Fide Reflections blog post that any concerns about James getting a big head were instantly dashed.

"She is no demanding diva. She is actually very humble and grateful about the success she has received. I remember when *Fifty Shades of Grey* was added to the Top 100 Erotica EBooks List on Amazon, E L was thrilled and maybe even a little floored by the response her book was getting."

And it was safe to say that in the meeting rooms and corporate offices of the major book publishing companies, the money crunchers were beginning to take a closer look at a genre that, in most cases, had been a consistent money maker but ultimately a stepchild to a roster of more serious works.

The upward spiral of *Fifty Shades of Grey* continued to climb into the latter months of 2011 and culminated in the book being nominated for honors at the Goodreads Choice Awards in the category of Best Romance.

"The nomination in early November caused a spike in interest from our members," Goodreads' Donaghy told CBS News. "The buzz kept growing as more people read the book and shared their reviews with their friends."

James helped grease the wheels at Goodreads in November and into early December when she visited the site on several occasions to answer fan questions.

"During November and December, those visits helped to maintain the momentum," Donaghy told CBS News. "The more people who read it, the more people heard about it, it just kept growing from there."

With the "out of nowhere" success of *Fifty Shades of Grey*, James was now being buffeted by the first real wave of cultural observation. Big-time pundits and unknown bloggers alike were lining up on both sides of what the book meant to women. Many thought *Fifty Shades of Grey* was a lightning rod of sexual liberation for women. Others dismissed it as a badly written and antiquated look at a misogynist putdown of women. There was the continued grumblings from the hardcore fan community that *Fifty Shades of Grey* was simply *Twilight* in ill-fitting sheep's clothing.

The websites Dear Author and Galley Cat were particularly aggressive in pointing out that *Fifty Shades* was a thinly disguised reworking of *Master of The Universe*, even going so far, in the case of Galley Cat, of comparing identical pages in both incarnations and noting that the similarity between the two versions stood at a robust 89 percent.

But all the conspiracy theories in the world could not prevent *Fifty Shades* from its march in popularity. Online figures on both Goodreads and Twitter indicated that the book's ground zero had been New York but that London, Los Angeles and Sydney had quickly fallen in line.

Normally very easygoing when it came to critics, James was most likely feeling a bit defensive, with the constant references to "mommy porn" perhaps being the most annoying label attached to her book.

"I can't own people's reactions to the book," the somewhat exasperated James told *Express And Star*.

But as she rang in the New Year with her family, James was aware that what had started out as simply an exercise in creative mind play had now morphed into something else. *Fifty Shades of Grey* was now out in the world in a significant way, touching lives and, yes, making a lot of money. As sales continued to climb and her notoriety began to grow, Erika simply could not get past the wonder of it all.

"My only dream was to see *Fifty Shades of Grey* in a bookshop," she told *Express And Star*. "This explosion of interest has taken me completely by surprise."

Surprise that, for James, was still going hand in hand with the inherent unease she continued to experience at being in the center of it all. "It's all pretty scary," she told *20/20*. "I really don't like the attention."

Amanda was more colorful in her description of E L James' unexpected success in a CNN World feature. "It snowballed to be honest with you. It happened so quickly. It's phenomenal. It was like a train that just didn't stop."

Up until this point, Erika had managed to keep her true identity a secret. The few who did know her identity had been as good as their word when they said they would keep her secret. Erika was quite content to let the alter ego of E L James carry the banner for her newfound avocation. But that would all change...

The day there was a knock on the door.

CHAPTER TEN
THE TRAIN LEFT THE STATION

Love them or hate them, you've got to give the British tabloid press their due. Because when it comes to tracking somebody down, they are quite good at that.

It had been determined that the mystery author had been hiding behind the pseudonym of E L James. From there it was a fairly short scouting trip through the world of fan fiction to discover that the author lived somewhere in the U.K. Soon they had an address.

And a name.

Erika Leonard found that her secret had been discovered shortly after the beginning of 2012 when a reporter for *The London Evening Standard* dropped by to ask if she were E L James? Erika was stunned and speechless at the reporter's question. Once she recovered her composure, how they found her out was of no immediate interest. What had her a bit upset was that her very tiny Australian publisher would now be overrun by the media. And that she would now be out in the public eye.

For better or worse, her secret was out. But, by

that point, any discomfort with her secret being discovered was easily balanced out by the fact that her success was already assured.

One needed only to check out the website likes and the glowing reviews from fans to know that *Fifty Shades* had found its market. Any doubts at that point were easily erased when she was updated on a regular basis by The Writer's Coffee Shop and the news would be all good.

It was a success that James continued to have a hard time coming to grips with, as she explained in a *Daily Record* feature. "I put it (the first book) out there quietly. I had a pen name. I thought I would just carry on working and write this stuff on the side."

By the conclusion of summer 2011, *Fifty Shades of Grey* had taken up residence in the personal psyche of countless women. Many had reread the book several times and were having withdrawals waiting anxiously for the follow-up book. Although a new publishing kid on the block, The Writer's Coffee Shop was a firm believer in striking while the iron was hot. Their intention had always been to get the second and third volumes of *Fifty Shades* out in a timely manner, a decision made all the more practical by the daily flood of emails, texts and blogs literally begging for the erotic saga to continue.

The publisher had made sure there would not be any copy-editing problems with the rest of the trilogy and, reportedly, were diligent in the cleaning up of typos and any lingering references to *Master of The Universe* that might have slipped through the cracks. Any bad feelings that might have surfaced with what was perceived as a lackluster editing job on the first book were all but forgiven amid James' praise for the new editing team.

And so on September 11, 2011 the second volume in the trilogy, *Fifty Shades Darker*, was published. News of the impending release of the second book had been put out well in advance and very much in line with how the first book had been publicized. The marketing template continued to work.

Like the first book, women gobbled up the continuation of the Christian/Anastasia odyssey in near manic fashion while critics remained mixed. As with the first book, *Darker* benefitted from loyal fan websites who continued to be effusive and, perhaps, less critical in their praise for James, one of their own who had made the big time.

Lara's Book Club stated, "*Fifty Shades Darker* delivers a certain darkness not seen in the first book." *The Oklahoma Daily* blasted the book, which it called "Just as mundane and ridiculous as the first novel." TVNZ said, "Like the first book, *Fifty Shades Darker* is full to the brim with Christian's and Ana's steamy antics that are sure to warm you on those cold winter nights." The Pattinson Post related that the book was "tough stuff that made me very emotional. I even shed a few tears."

James was grateful for the positive notices and had learned quickly to ignore the less-kind reviews. Her feeling was that she would not be derailed by critics. "I am very self-critical," she told *Bookish Temptations*. "But I feel that as long as people are reading your work, you must be doing something right."

The response to *Fifty Shades Darker* had

succeeded in elevating James' work to the level of "critic proof." The story had struck a nerve, an emotion that went beyond any perception of questionable writing and pedestrian storytelling.

"I think I've tapped into something," said a completely at a loss James in conversation with Woman And Home. "But to this day I don't know exactly what."

With the *Fifty Shades* series now in the can, James soon returned to the many other creative irons she had in the fire.

"I have quite a few ideas at the moment," she told Awesomeness. "It freaks me out that I have to pick one out to work on. I have virtual Post-it notes on my computer and 12 different storylines going at the moment."

But while James would insist that her other projects were not like Fifty Shades, the websites were alive with the notion that the author was planning to revisit the world of Christian and Anastasia, either as a retelling of the tale from Christian's perspective or a whole new story. Whatever the truth was, in the public's mind, the only thing that mattered was *Fifty Shades Darker* and where the story would ultimately go.

The marketing of *Fifty Shades Darker* mirrored the approach of *Fifty Shades of Grey*; lots of online blogging and essentially playing to her fan base in the romance fiction community. The latter was largely taken up with another blog book tour that ran from October 3 to October 14. Although still working on a television project, James easily made time in her day to willingly do interviews and posts with the all-important websites. The questions remained pretty much the same as with the press go-around on the first book. But now there were a lot of queries about how the trilogy would ultimately play out. James teased her questioners with vague asides but was keeping the particulars of her storyline to herself.

James did explain during the blog tour that she was definitely seeing a change in the character of Christian as the storyline progressed.

"I do think that Christian has become a little more open minded in *Fifty Shades Darker*," she told Book That Thing. "He's more willing to try something new and he has allowed himself to let go of some of his iron control."

Word of mouth about the middle-aged British mom and her erotic books that were heating up the e-book industry was moving out of the romance fiction websites and making inroads into the mainstream press. And those outlets were quick to latch onto the very story angles that had long ago had their run on the Internet. Their approach would inevitably be lighthearted and bemused in tone and, perhaps, just a shade condescending. But the important thing remained that the E L James phenomena was showing signs of branching out into the mainstream.

And giving birth to the infamous tag "mommy porn."

Where that phrase came from was anybody's guess. But the origin most cited was *The New York Times*. Whoever took credit, the fact remained that the mainstream press had found the ideal way to explain what E L James and *Fifty Shades* was all about.

After hearing that catchphrase one too many

times, James reluctantly threw up her hands during an interview with CBC. "In this world of 140 characters, it's all kind of tidy. It's not what I would have called it."

James would constantly be at odds with the phrase, fighting back as best she could with an earnest acknowledgment that her books were actually a fantasy love story that happened to contain a lot of sex.

James continued to bask in the sheer enormity of what her tales had brought to women in terms of being sexually open to their desires, the improbability of e-book publishing success on a massive level and the fact that untold financial gain was in the offing. More and more of her time and thoughts were now occupied with being a best-selling author of major proportions.

Once word had gotten out about her other life and her mounting success, James had become the office celebrity, subject to good-natured ribbing and support. James got through those days with good cheer and low-key acceptance of her office mates' praise. But beyond those light moments, she had discovered that her day job had quickly become an afterthought.

So it came as little surprise that, not long after the release of *Fifty Shades Darker*, she quit her television job to devote her time to her career and her family, with the full blessing of Niall and her children. It was a bittersweet decision according to her interview with All About You.

"I kind of miss my mates where I used to work."

Niall was fully supportive of his wife's decision but in a commentary written for the *Guardian*, he did admit to a certain amount of concern. "I felt a twinge of panic when she told me she was giving up her job.

She was the only one of us with a regular income. But I thought (with the way the book was selling) we should be ok for six months or so and I'll probably have landed an episode of something by then."What she did not miss was the long rides on the tube, the long hours sitting at a desk juggling numbers and the time spent away from a new avocation that she had grown to love.

Her family continued to be a rock in supporting and dealing with her newfound notoriety. Niall was totally behind James, his good humor and encouragement continued to be a major factor in her dealing with fame. To her children, James was still mum and they were low-key in acknowledging what she was up to in her writing life.

With the final installment of the *Fifty Shades* trilogy now looming on the horizon, James was faced with some uncertainty with where, or even if, the franchise should go next. Countless readers had already begun Internet chatter on more *Fifty Shades* stories and, in particular, the entire *Fifty Shades* storyline told from Christian's perspective. James acknowledged that such a turn on the original story was possible, and, in an interview with *Express And Star*, painted a rather idyllic picture of how it all might play out.

"I'd love to be sitting in my leggings, my Uggs and my old oversized sweatshirt, creating another Christian Grey trilogy."

There were also the continued hints being dropped that James was currently working on a non-*Fifty Shades* story. But the reality was that with all the promotion and marketing duties surrounding the first two books, James' writing output had slowed to a near halt. The author was most likely torn between the ego boost she derived from being in the spotlight and the pure desire of sitting down and doing the work.

At a particularly hectic point on the promotion trail, James told *USA Today*, "I'd rather be at home writing."

James finished out the year with a handful of interviews and press obligations. But if her tweets to friends and fans were any indication, quiet times at home with friends, good drink and good cheer in their patio garden was part and parcel of her time away from the spotlight, as was the occasional night out at favorite restaurants.

Into 2012, both author and publisher were gearing up for the final chapter of the *Fifty Shades* odyssey. While the particulars of E L James' contract with The Writer's Coffee Shop remained confidential, the consensus among observers was that the author's obligation to the publisher would end with the release of *Fifty Shades Freed*. Whatever the future might bring, The Writer's Coffee Shop was intent on going out in style.

To celebrate the release of *Fifty Shades Freed*, publisher and author flew to New York for a proper send-off for the final chapter. The mood as the final book hit the e-book superhighway was equal parts joy and melancholy. It had been a hugely successful ride that had changed the fortunes of both author and publisher.

James was like a fish out of water at the party, alternately shy and appreciative but finally caught up in the notion that the extravagance of the party reflected something much bigger on the horizon. She was particularly excited at the rock star-like reception she received at the launch of *Fifty Shades Freed.*

"I think it was the screeching," she recalled of that night in a *Newsday* conversation. "I felt like Brad Pitt. It was extraordinary."

And it was also a flashback to the first conversation she had with her agent Valerie Hoskins. "I think the first thing I said to Valerie, very tongue in cheek of course, was that 'I do not want to be famous.' I can't think of anything worse."

That night in New York, fame was very much the author's companion.

Jenny Pedroza from The Writer's Coffee Shop related to the author that the publication party for *Fifty Shades Freed* would be the starting point for major mainstream interest. "It all started with the publication party. There was that big piece in *The New York Times* and the books started getting on best-seller lists. At that point the big publishers were contacting all of us."

James jumped right into the expected *Fifty Shades Freed* blog tour that went from January 23 to February 2. It was an easy time in which James schmoozed with fans and friends in the web community. There was a sense of loyalty about the websites. They had been there from the beginning. She owed them much. But there was also a sense of finality about these interactions.

There was the growing mainstream interest to contend with. While early on she had been willing to do any and all press and had been grateful for the attention, she was slowly coming to grips with the fact that there was just not enough time in the day. Cynics in the fan fiction community, if blogs and tweets were to be believed, were chaffing at the idea of one of their own outgrowing them and moving on to greener pastures. To be certain, some of the responses were born of jealousy and nothing else.

What would happen next was anybody's guess.

James had taken the step of acquiring high-powered literary agent Valerie Hoskins the previous year. Like other aspects of her short career, it had not been easy. She had previously approached two other top London literary agents to represent her and had been summarily rejected. Hoskins recalled in an interview with *The Sunday Times* that James did not take kindly to rejection.

"She felt hurt at the time and so had stopped looking."

At that point, Niall came to her aid. Niall had long been a client of Hoskins, whose agency specializes in representing film and television writers. The agent had a policy of not considering new books or new authors for clients but, when Niall confided in his agent regarding his wife's woes and the need for some advice, Hoskins agreed to take a meeting with the author.

"We met and we got on well immediately," said Hoskins to *The Sunday Times*. Hoskins did her homework and discovered that the *Fifty Shades* books were doing amazing business for an e-book and so she went against policy and signed James up.

The announcement that James had signed with a big-time agent furthered the growing speculation that *Fifty Shades* would eventually make its way to the movie screen and that the rights to the first three books might well make their way to a large mainstream publisher.

Hoskins had tagged along to the New York release party for *Fifty Shades Freed* and was immediately thrust into the middle of U.S. publishers' surging interest, fielding several offers and doing yeoman's duty as James' go between.

What was known was that the buzz created around the final installment of the story catapulted the already massive sales of the books to an even higher level.

Reviews remained mixed. It went without saying that fans were more inclined to be more favorable in their assessment than hardboiled critics. But James' attempt at bringing the entire *Fifty Shades* saga full circle proved challenging for even James' diehard "can do no wrong" supporters.

The reviewer for Guilty Pleasures indicated that "Ms. James really does cover a lot of ground and sometimes it all seemed a little surreal." TVNZ said, "I have to say that, by the third book, the sex scenes started to get, darest I say it, a little boring." The Sinful Books reviewer offered, "I think James was trying to flesh out the story and give it more depth than just sex. It was basically the same story but the story remained interesting."

There was the notion that *Fifty Shades* might ultimately have been better served as a two-book storyline and that the way the final book concluded was a sign that the story had become too cumbersome.

When the numbers were finally crunched, the final push by *Fifty Shades Freed* quite literally pushed the series into best-seller status. Never a priority, the print-on-demand element of The Writer's Coffee Shop had always been sluggish and actual hard copies of the Australian publisher's editions would blossom into true collector's items. By early 2012, an estimated 7,000 copies had actually been sold.

But the true magnitude of *Fifty Shades'* popularity played itself out in the continued sense of privacy and freedom from judgment that women felt in buying the books under the cover of e-book secrecy. And it was that element of the brave new book buying world that had an impact on the final tally of e-book sales.

250,000 copies.

CHAPTER ELEVEN
THE IDES OF MARCH

Two hundred and fifty thousand. A quarter of a million. Anyway you sliced it, the number was big. The number was magic.

It was also an irresistible bait to dangle before U.S. publishers who were lining up to dance with E L James.

According to reports, by the early weeks of 2012, several U.S. publishers were in a spirited bidding war for the rights to print copies of the already wildly successful series. Quickly it became evident that the clear frontrunner was Vintage Books. Vintage, an imprint of the powerhouse Random House/Knopf/Doubleday Publishing Group, was known for publishing more literary, darest we say, highbrow literature. However, the publishing giant's interest was piqued when Vintage Publisher Anne Messitte was given a copy by a colleague at Random House.

"Within a day, I was socializing with some moms at my kids' school and they were chatting about the books," she told *The New York Times*.

Messitte's curiosity grew when she downloaded

and read *Fifty Shades of Grey*. She immediately downloaded the second book. She instantly saw the potential. Messitte began to monitor the divamoms.com website and was impressed with the passion of the discussions surrounding James' books. Through Divamoms, she found contact information for James and her agent and, on January 24, she met with them and outlined her proposal for acquiring the books.

"I really wanted to make an offer," she told *The New York Times*. "I told them I had some very strong ideas on how to republish the books."

After engaging in "the most complex deal I had ever worked on," Vintage finally triumphed in a competitive negotiating process over four other publishers.

But the conservative publisher needed only check the best-seller charts to know that making what was reported in *The New York Times* to be a seven-figure offer was the right decision.

For the week ending March 3, *Fifty Shades of Grey* was sitting at No. 1 on *The New York Times* best-seller list for e-book fiction and No. 3 on Amazon's Best-seller list.

Literally hours after the chart listings were made public, James had signed on the bottom line with Vintage. Vintage executives and James' agent took turns praising the deal.

"We're making a statement that this is bigger than one genre," Messitte said in a *New York Times* piece. "The people who are reading this are not only people who read romance. It's gone much broader than that."

James' agent, Valerie Hoskins, who immediately

jumped from negotiating the Vintage deal to haggling over film and foreign language rights, also praised the deal to *The New York Times*, couching her comments in social as well as financial terms.

"I think it can only get bigger in terms of its success," she said. "One of the things about this is that, in the 21st century, women have the ability to read this kind of material without people knowing what they're reading."

But it remained for James to cut to the heart of the deal which, in a statement, centered on her readers.

"I've heard from so many readers who are trying to find these books in bookstores and libraries. It is gratifying to know that they will soon be widely available in the U.S. and around the world."

News of the Vintage signing was bittersweet. The Writer's Coffee Shop reportedly received royalties of book sales for the next three years from the deal that would make the fledgling company a financially sound publisher for some time to come and would allow the company to put more into the marketing of other deserving authors. But the deal also effectively put an end to the company's attachment to the *Fifty Shades* books.

Amanda Hayward was upbeat and somewhat philosophical in a conversation with 720 Sydney. "It's good that it started out as an e-book. It shows that this is definitely the way of the future."

Pedroza echoed her partner's sentiments while waxing nostalgic in an interview with the author. "We are so excited to see what she is continuing to do with her writing career. And we are truly grateful to have been at the start of it all."

The Writer's Coffee Shop would go on to benefit from their getting in on the ground floor of *Fifty Shades*. The notoriety brought a flood of worthy manuscripts to the attention of the company and, knowing a good thing when they see it, the publisher was quick to jump on a new romance/erotic book series from Sherri Hayes, whose second book in the series, *Need*, was very much in keeping with the tone and vibe of *Fifty Shades*. While nowhere near the sales of James' books, author Hayes' series did quite well in the now all-important e-book world.

Behind the scenes at Vintage, yet another round of editing was going on to get *Fifty Shades* mainstream publishing worthy. Vintage did a very quick edit while James, likewise, went over *Darker* and *Freed* with the proverbial fine-tooth comb. She would often acknowledge the feverish pace of those final edits in the face of an insane demand for the physical books.

Vintage would waste no time in capitalizing on their investment. On March 9, mere days after inking the deal, Vintage released all three books in the *Fifty Shades* series in digital format.

How well the books would do in hard copy form remained a legitimate question within the publishing house. The first print run of *Fifty Shades of Grey* had been pegged at 250,000 copies. So nobody was more amazed than the decision makers at Vintage when pre-orders of the book began rolling in from retail stores to the tune of 450,000 copies. Amazed and encouraged, Vintage immediately bumped the first print run to 500,000 copies.

Early in April, the first paperback editions under the Vintage banner hit bookstores. It was a bold, quick strike on Vintage's part and a bit of a risky one in that the target audience for the books had already read them in one form or another.

However, the naysayers had not counted on the continued excitement surrounding an impending mainstream publisher for the books and the notion that, for many, they could now own a hard print copy of their favorite books.

Spearheaded by the idea of finally being able to go into an actual bookstore and purchase a copy, along with the new liberation that entailed, Vintage's gamble paid off. By late April, the three *Fifty Shades* books occupied the top three spots on *The New York Times* best-seller list, the first time in the history of the list that three books by the same author had occupied the top three spots.

Vintage knew they had a tiger by the tail and immediately designed a marketing program directed at the summer/beach reading crowd. Their tagline: Reading for pleasure has a whole new meaning. Admittedly, while the folks at Vintage were working overtime to make *Fifty Shades* a mammoth success, James and her books had long since passed the point where a marketing campaign was truly necessary. The books had, for quite some time, been selling themselves without any help.

But the campaign worked in keeping interest at a fever pitch and well into July, the *Fifty Shades* books remained a fixture at the top of the best-seller list. That same month Vintage proudly announced that James' books had brought the company a total of $145 million in U.S. revenue alone. The mind boggled at what the financial gain would be when the revenue of the 41 other countries who purchased foreign language rights was factored in.

Given the enormity of the deal and the fact that, to the majority of the world E L James was still unknown, press coverage by the mainstream press used the rags to riches angle as a jumping off point to talk about the dollars and cents of it all. In fact, no less a publication than *The Wall Street Journal* devoted an entire story to statistics breaking down the sales of paperbacks and e-books, the total number of copies sold and the profits of Vintage.

At a time when most of the news surrounding the publishing industry had been bleak, *Fifty Shades of Grey* had laid claim to the feel-good story of the decade; a story that seemed to have a very long way to run.

Money was very much a part of this equation.

And James was not immune from the speculation as to how much she was now worth. By summer, the niche website Celebrity Net Worth was trumpeting the fact that James' current net worth was $15 million. *The Daily Mail* broke it down even further, stating that James, based on her book royalty rate and the fact that she had, almost certainly, paid off her advance, was now making $1 million a week from an average weekly sale of 1 million books and e-books.

The total disbelief of it all was not lost on James who, in a May 2012 conversation with *USA Today*, acknowledged that she was mentally pinching herself at every turn. "It's very strange. It's just that everything has happened so quickly.

"It's like it's happening to somebody else."

CHAPTER TWELVE
SUCH A DEAL

James celebrated New Year's Eve in the bosom of family and friends. It had been a long, miraculous year in which her life was forever changed. She was hoping for a relatively quiet, uneventful night. But that was too much to ask for.

"On New Year's Eve I received an email inquiring about the film rights," she told *The Daily Mail*. "I nearly fell off my chair. Then I got another one and another one."

James was smart enough to know how things work.

First you get the book deal. Then you get the movie deal. In the case of *Fifty Shades*, the author found that her agent, Valerie Hoskins, had simultaneously been fielding offers from interested studios while locking down the particulars of the deal with Vintage.

The author had to admit that she had some trepidation about *Fifty Shades* making its way to the silver screen. "I'm really worried about that (a movie adaptation of her book)," she admitted to a packed house during a Q&A session in London. "A book is such a personal experience between the author and the reader and the books are almost always better than the movies. I did have some concerns. But then I thought, 'sod it,' when am I going to have the chance to work on a Hollywood movie?"

The consensus was that a March 10 article in *The New York Times*, coupled with the deal with Vintage, had been the catalyst in kicking open the Hollywood floodgates. In point of fact, several studios had already gotten wind of the *Fifty Shades* explosion and were on the phone with Hoskins to get the inside track on a film deal. But the agent was insistent that there be a book deal in place before there was any serious discussion of a movie.

And rather than go the preferred route of hiring an expert in the arena of big money film deals, James and Hoskins decided that they were more than capable of conducting film business without outside help. Another element of their rather unorthodox approach was to make creative demands, something unheard of when a deal involved somebody perceived to have little clout or reputation. And rather than simply throw *Fifty Shades* out to the whims of the highest bidder, the new power duo made it clear that money would not be the overriding factor.

Not surprisingly, every heavy hitter in Hollywood immediately stepped up to the plate. They included Warner Bros., Paramount, Universal/Focus Features, New Regency, Mandate, Sony and Lionsgate/Summit. The all-star lineup of producers and studio higher-ups willing to take a swing included Greg Silverman, Rob Friedman, Brad Grey, Lorenzo di Bonaventura, Arnon Milchan, Neal Moritz, Brian Grazer, Todd Garner,

Adam Shankman, Amy Pascal and Scott Rudin.

Some of the aforementioned suitors even attempted to get in on the action early, with HBO offering a January offer that was declined and Sony and New Regency making early bids that were also turned down.

Typical of the game-playing employed in Hollywood, one unidentified producer who reportedly turned down a chance to pitch, told *The Guardian*, "The material is really not any good. There are a lot of producers involved in the auction who you can't imagine having any passion for the material but see it as a pure business opportunity."

James was initially under the impression that she would observe the film deal proceedings from afar and get daily updates from her agent in the States. But Hoskins felt that it would be best for her charge to be on Hollywood's home turf so that the author could meet the studio representatives face to face and better gauge their intentions for her books.

"I thought the best way we could make a decision, because of the level of involvement she wanted to have, was to come out here (Hollywood)," Hoskins explained to deadline.com. "She would see the whites of their eyes and then make a decision based on the people as much as their offers."

In preliminary discussions between author and agent, James made it clear that she was not in it just for a big payday and to then let the studio do what they will with her books. A collaborative spirit was very much on James' mind. She was insistent that she have a voice in the script, cast, director, locations, marketing and movie trailer approval and that any indication of a lack of same would be considered a deal breaker, although she was insistent that she was not going into negotiations with an eye toward being a control freak.

"We always said that if we didn't find a fit, we'd pack our bags and go home," she told *Entertainment Weekly*.

One element of the negotiations that was troubling to James was the notion of having to talk at length with male film executives about her books' sex scenes.

"You have no idea how embarrassing it is to discuss my fantasies in a room full of male Hollywood executives," she related to an enthralled London event audience. "I can't even tell you how cringe-worthy that is. I never expected men to read this at all."

Midway through March, James and Hoskins landed in Southern California and began a whirlwind of days in which she took meetings on the lots of the world's biggest studios. For James, meeting with big names at big studios was a nonstop adrenaline rush of discussions that centered more on the creative aspects than the financial figures. At the conclusion of the initial round of meetings, James was exhausted... but also very excited.

Because on Friday, March 24, the last studio had made their pitch. Now it was time for James to make a decision. The author and her agent went into complete lockdown over the weekend, imposing radio or any other news media outlet silence to avoid rumors or alleged "breaking news" that might possibly influence their decision. Nobody talks money in Hollywood unless at the business end of a gun, but the speculation was running rampant that all the studios had agreed to varying degrees to James' terms and that some financial offers were higher than others.

Monday, March 26 brought the announcement people both in and out of the industry had been waiting for. Universal/Focus Features had sealed the deal for a reported $5 million and all of James' creative demands.

There was some grumbling, as there always is among jilted suitors, that other offers that were rejected had offered more money. But Universal/Focus' willingness to give James input into a director, script and casting, as well as the dogged pursuit of Universal/Focus executives Donna Langley and Jeb Brody, ultimately tipped the scales. James was also enamored of Focus Features' track record in dealing with what many considered "difficult properties" such as *Lost In Translation* and *The Pianist*.

But behind the scenes, there were cautionary predictions, and maybe a few sour grapes, regarding the possibilities of a *Fifty Shades* movie. Many unnamed people in the industry felt that a literal translation of the *Fifty Shades* saga would most certainly run afoul of the motion pictures' ratings board. In the same vein, others speculated that the sex scenes were too graphic to faithfully capture on film. Still another warned that it was a numbers game and that, quite simply, a large percentage of people who bought the book would not be inclined to see the movie. As always, it would remain to be seen.

Meanwhile...

In a celebratory state, James remained cautiously

optimistic about her book-to-film experience, as she explained in an *Examiner* piece.

"So far it's been good fun and I hope it stays that way."

It was drinks all around and fine food as James and Hoskins celebrated their victory. Then it was time for James to wing home and to attempt some quiet time with Niall and her children. But the author knew that time would be short-lived. Because with major book and movie deals came further responsibilities in getting out there and meeting the masses. James was not putting her passport away just yet.

She sensed that she would soon need it again.

CHAPTER THIRTEEN
DAYS ON THE ROAD

And as it turned out, she would be right.

Hoping to get in some quiet time with her family, James was literally greeted at the doorstep with the news that her first major book tour of the U.S. was being put together to start in late April and to continue through the second week of May. The *Fifty Shades* tour would concentrate on the East Coast and include stops in Miami, Chicago, Boston, New Haven, Washington D.C., New Jersey and a three-day stint in New York City.

The tour was playing to James' strengths and sales. It would be touching down in areas that had shown the earliest and most vociferous support for her books. With James very much an author who liked to reward loyalty, it was a comfortable fit for her introduction to her public.

And by book tour standards, it was shaping up as a lavish production. The masterminds behind the tour felt that a three-ring circus, filled to the brim with fun-loving notions, was in keeping with the tone of *Fifty Shades* and the easygoing nature of the author.

Mixed in with the expected bookstore signings

were a number of ticketed luncheon/lecture/Q&A events in which fans would pay for the privilege of a meet and greet with their favorite author.

James' family was understanding and supportive of the author having to get on the road and support her books; although if sales were any indication, just about everybody on the planet already owned them.

The book tour was also shaping up as a true test of James' ability to handle a large audience. She had admitted on several occasions to being shy and a bit uneasy in large crowds but, at the launch party for *Fifty Shades Freed* in New York, appeared to handle the throng and the adulation well.

James was assured that the events would be well-choreographed, in which she would regale screaming and appreciative fans with many of the stories she had told countless times before and would sign endless amounts of books and do some press at each stop. She felt she was up to the task and so, late in April, she kissed and hugged her family goodbye and flew back to the states and the first stop on the tour.

April 29: Miami.

The first stop on the tour was a fair barometer of what James would face in the coming days. The scheduled evening lecture/Q&A/signing had sold out in record time. Not wanting to disappoint her fans, James hastily arranged a morning book signing at a store in nearby Coral Gables. Word of mouth continued to be her constant companion when, with short notice and very little publicity, more than 500 fans engulfed the store, waving her books in the air and screaming her name. The excitement and praise for the author was palpable. James was engaging in this first brush with her public and was confident that her first big appearance later that evening would go equally well.

It would be more of the same that night at a hotel ballroom where James entertained an estimated 600 attendees. The event had been done up in a mixture of bawdy and circus. Banners featuring various *Fifty Shades* catchphrases were everywhere, as were waiters dressed to the nines, flitting around offering dainty colored drinks to the attendees.

Any hint of nervousness seemed to vanish as she came across as warm, candid and clever throughout the evening. This was the bookstore equivalent of rock star treatment and James handled it all with grace, a smile never far from her face.

On this first stop, James would learn the reality of this level of celebrity; which was if you did not leave the stage and immediately hide in your hotel room, you were still onstage in a matter of speaking.

James was on her way down a hotel hallway after the event, hoping to unwind in the hotel bar, when she was suddenly surrounded by a group of women who, after attending the event, were on the hunt for more *Fifty Shades* experiences. They were excited and giddy, requesting photos, a bit of one-on-one chat time and a few extra autographs that had not been part of the event limit. James was a good sport about it all— right up until the point where she felt a need to escape. She turned on her heels and walked briskly to the hotel bar.

She entered the bar and a roar of excitement greeted her. It turned out that a couple of book clubs were in the bar, dissecting James' appearance. She had been instantly recognized and once again surrounded. James was once again the perfect host, repeating the same process of photos and autographs with a tired smile that was verging on forced.

James would good-naturedly explain to *Entertainment Weekly* what her life as a famous author on tour had become. "I'm now, full-time, someone who gets carted around and thrown in front of people."

April 30: Chicago.

The Standard Club. Paid tickets bought the more than 400 women in attendance cocktails, munchies and the prerequisite meet and greet and book signing. James seemed to be quickly rounding into shape as she basked in the adulation. A short introduction by James, the Q&A and the book signing. And, oh yes, the applause and screams. At this point, James could sense what questions were coming and what people wanted to know. She would be alternately straightforward, funny and continually blown away by what her story had wrought. And in increasing numbers she would hear stories about what her books had done for the women, in and out of the bedroom... and was touched.

"It's really exhausting and I find all the hoopla around it extraordinary," she remarked to *USA Today* at one point in the tour. "But it's great to meet people who really love the books."

James left Chicago in a good place. Up next?

May 1: Boston.

Boston proved a test of fans' endurance. A substantial downpour the day before threatened to dampen enthusiasm and attendance for James' Burlington signing. But the rain let up and literally hundreds of fans lined up to meet James. A humorous aside for the author was that the chef at the hotel where she was staying concocted a chocolate-and-fruit-filled replica of the *Fifty Shades* cover. Once she stopped laughing, James was totally appreciative of the gesture.

May 2: New Haven, Connecticut.

The author's appearance at The Omni New Haven Hotel was shaping up as the biggest stop on the book tour so far. Reportedly more than a thousand tickets had been snapped up for the Q&A/interview/book signing/cocktail hour extravaganza.

James had been amazed and heartened by the response so far and there was a broad smile on her face as she waited offstage for her introduction. What she had not counted on was the sheer emotion of this experience in the limelight finally catching up to her. She described what happened in a 9 News item.

"I went into a room and there were about a thousand women there. They all started applauding and I started to cry."

Once she stopped crying, James told the audience, "This is really fucking phenomenal. I didn't foresee this at all."

James caught a train from New Haven for the relatively short trip to Philadelphia. On the ride, she found the time to call home and check on her children.

"I missed them," she confessed to newjersey.com and *The Record*. "They were just telling me about their day and stuff. That's absolutely how it should be."

May 3: Philadelphia.

This signing was vintage hysteria. The long lines of fans. The appreciation, the applause, the "thank you's for improving my life." The book signing. More "Laters Babe" E L James than you could shake a stick at. Writer's cramp. James a good sport to the end. It was all good.

May 4: Washington D.C.

Anyone speculating just how big the whole *Fifty Shades* mania had become easily had their question answered during the author's stopover at the Bethesda Barnes & Noble. James was ushered into the store with an entourage that included her agent, publicist and, last but certainly not least, one of the higher-ups of her U.S. publishing company. Inside the store proper, clerks and store managers were roaming the aisles, walkie-talkies in hand, sending and receiving information about how many books and in what fashion they would be signed and where the line formed. Anybody who had trouble figuring out the latter need only look down at the arrows on the floor pointing in the right direction. James was her usual appreciative self as she sat down at the signing table, dwarfed by the stacks of books rising up all around her. There were 2,000 copies of her books on hand. And before the night was over, she would sign them all. And then some.

Things were getting a bit chaotic in the rules department at this signing. The bookstore had set up definite guidelines, which quickly crumbled. A limit of three books only to be signed was overruled by requests to sign T-shirts and other non-book items and to pose for pictures. Through it all, James was conspicuous by the smile on her face as she accommodated each and every request to the frustration of store employees who played by the rules.

Following the Washington event, James took a few days off to relax and enjoy the bits of America she could manage when she was not being drawn into last-minute, and quite necessary, media obligations.

And, as she would later relate in a *GQ* piece, during this time she marveled at the extreme candor she was greeted with by her fans. "One woman said to me, 'I had my first spanking two weeks ago.' I mean, what's the appropriate reply when somebody tells you that?"

Next stop, the Big Apple.

May 7: Long Island.

A big entry into the Big Apple. The Carlyle on the Green ballroom was packed with more than 400 ardent fans who had shelled out big bucks for a lunch/Q&A/book signing three-way experience. The women were dressed in their finery, enthusiastic and living for the moment when they could have an audience with the person who seemingly singlehandedly had changed their lives.

Merchandizing of the *Fifty Shades* concept had quickly seeped into the book tour and was extremely blatant at the Long Island event. As those in attendance lined up to get their books signed, they were greeted with a literal Middle Eastern marketplace of impulse buying, tied to varying degrees, of the *Fifty Shades* brand. Among the items being sold were erotic-themed necklaces and various shades of high-priced vibrators. All apparently done with the approval of the event organizers. Aka the author.

What had become evident by the time the tour hit Long Island was that the particulars of the experience were now being tightly controlled. Rather than real interaction during the Q&A, questions were now being pre-screened with only the softballs that James had answered seemingly forever being tossed up for her to hit. But, in the coverage of the event by *Newsday*, something of minor newness did emerge.

Responding to the question of what she had learned by writing the books, the author responded, "I hate being on television, I have a pretty good sense of humor and I'm not very different from other women in their fantasies."

It seemed that James was never less than accommodating during the Long Island event but, according to coverage by WABC, there were, perhaps, signs that exhaustion was beginning to set in. Normally very press-friendly, the author insisted on no interviews tied to this event. She further said that she did not want cameras present. None of which stopped her fans from snapping away with their cell phones.

FYI: That same day James did a free book signing at a nearby bookstore for those who could not afford the hefty ticket price.

May 8: New Jersey.

The spectacle of an author of note coming to New Jersey was the big lure once people got past the inherent impact of the books. Some fans reportedly camped out overnight to get a good spot for the event. The book signing went the way they all had. From the look on James' face, she was obviously reveling in the adulation. At one point she cracked wise about how her signing hand was not getting tired. The attendees, as only Jerseyites can be, were effusive and very real in their interaction with James. And that may ultimately turn out to be the bottom line. People were festive and in the spirit of the author and the books that had influenced their thoughts and lives. On the surface, it was all very deep and philosophical. But in the trenches, where the real people dwell, New Jersey proved that *Fifty Shades* could be very festive and real.

One attendee in particular tugged at James' heartstrings when she informed the author of a recent series of chemotherapy treatments and that *Fifty Shades* had gone a long way toward helping her through the blues. James said, "God bless" and wished her the best.

James found some time during her New York stay to visit the offices of Vintage. If Facebook is any indication, she mixed and mingled with higher-ups and staff alike. She was legitimately grateful for the job Vintage had been doing on her behalf and it was smiles all around.

At this point in the book tour, James was starting to fall victim to the logistics of it all as she explained to newjersey.com. "Sleep. That's what I would like next. I would pay good money for sleep. I'd like to be able to unpack my suitcase. I haven't been able to do that yet."

May 10: New York City.

Day one of a two-day extravaganza to bring the tour to a conclusion at a Barnes & Noble outlet. And James' first real encounter with dissent. A small but vocal group had stationed themselves outside the entrance to the event, waving protest signs and screaming that the *Fifty Shades* books were pornography. The protestors were largely ignored as fans walked into the event. They saw things differently.

Sex specialist Dr. Logan Levkoff was brought in to moderate a Q&A with the author. The attempt appeared to veer off into a somewhat intellectual give and take on the sexual politics advanced by the *Fifty Shades* trilogy. But the shrieks and screams that regularly interrupted James' remarks quickly moved the event from serious to Beatlemania levels of adulation. The books were signed. The pleasantries and praise were exchanged. Ever the trooper, James was nothing less than cordial and giving to her audience.

But one could possibly sense that she was mentally counting down the moments until she could jump on a plane and go home.

May 11: New York City.

The last day. The last hotel room. The last strange bed. The last stop on the tour was bigger than life. The Willow Bridge Country Club packed them in. If you believed the breathless press reports, thousands were turned away. Divamoms' guiding light Lyss Stern ram-rodded yet another fairly rote interview, alternately outrageously funny but always by the book and on the clock. James hit the pre-screened questions from the audience out of the park.

Among those was a chirpy response to how she felt about improving her readers' sex lives. "I don't know how I feel about that. I think it's wonderful." And then there was the question of how she separates celebrity from real life. "It's very easy," she told the audience and was reported by *The Harrison Patch*. "I turn around and look at my living room and it's a mess. I have to do laundry. I don't have any difficulty distinguishing between the two."

Books were signed. Thanks and hugs all around.

Lots of people hawking various bits of *Fifty Shades* stuff. Lots of people hitching a ride on the gravy train. It was all too exploitive and obvious but fans of James were taking it all as good sport and part and parcel of the spectacle. And that made it all okay.

E L James' U.S. book tour had only been two weeks. But beyond the hype, hoopla and the often three-ring circus nature, for James one thing had been made abundantly clear: She had seen the faces of the people who were responding to her books. And she liked what she saw.

CHAPTER FOURTEEN
FIFTY SHADES OF BUZZ

James was thrilled to be home. She craved the quiet and would spend several days reacquainting herself with her family and indulging in just plain quiet time.

And of course the much prayed for sleep.

The reality of *Fifty Shades* would have to wait. But as she was about to find out, it would not wait very long.

Ever since she signed the movie deal, every conceivable formal and informal news outlet was on fire with the latest rumors surrounding the film adaptation of *Fifty Shades*. Any person with a modicum of celebrity was suddenly rumored to be in talks regarding the first film. The first to make headlines was Angelina Jolie who, according to press reports, was being courted to direct the film. There was the inevitable "she's interested" and "she's not interested" but finally nothing definitive.

Fan websites chimed in with casting suggestions that ran the gamut of Robert Pattinson, Ian Somerhalder, Taylor Kitsch and countless others for the role of Christian, and Scarlett Johansson, Kristen Stewart, Emmy Rossum and seemingly every young and vulnerable-looking starlet for the role of Anastasia. Fantasy pairings were also in the suggestion box; the one getting the most juice being real-life lovers Pattinson and Stewart in the title roles.

James addressed that particular pairing at several events by saying "ugh."

But through no fault of her own, James was also fanning the fires of speculation, seemingly every time the question was asked. As quoted in Celebuzz, she deflected the notion of casting when she stated, "We are so far away from casting the *Fifty* films. No one is ruled out. No one is ruled in."

However, during a July speaking engagement in London, she surprised her audience when she stated, for the first time, and reported by London Guru, "I am mum on who should play the characters. But I do have four people in mind to play each character."

Enterprising journalists took the opportunity to approach every age-appropriate actor and actress with the question of whether they would be interested in *Fifty Shades*. The bemused responses ranged from a simple "yes" to "no" to "I haven't read the books yet." Their responses were essentially non-stories but in the tabloid world, they were immediately good for a headline and a paragraph or two.

Easily the most legitimate and, yes, most self-serving attempt to hitch a ride on the *Fifty Shades* wagon was the media/tweet blitz by author/screenwriter Bret Easton Ellis, who was almost apoplectic in his public desire to script the film.

One particular tweet, picked up by numerous news outlets, including *The New York Post*, said, "I'm putting myself out there to write the movie adaptation of *Fifty Shades of Grey.*" Ellis was no stranger to the dark side, having created a legendary stir with his novel *American Psycho*. "I think Christian and Anastasia are potentially great cinematic characters."

Ellis would continue his barrage by suggesting Scarlett Johansson for the role of Anastasia and his good buddy director David Cronenberg (actually not a bad choice given his dark credentials and his underappreciated erotic film *Crash*). Ellis' lobbying would elicit no comment from James' camp. And with good reason.

The film was going nowhere without the right producers, the hunt for which was now an active search in Hollywood going into June.

James temporarily put aside *Fifty Shades* to celebrate the recent success of her husband Niall, whose young adult thriller *Crusher* had found a home with Random House in June and would be released in September as the first in a reported three-book deal. It was not the obvious nepotism call that most people jumped to. But James did have a hand in it.

Niall had long been itching to write a novel and in November 2011, he took the plunge at his wife's suggestion to write a novel in a month as part of an event held by the website National Novel Writing Month, which stages events in which novels are written in 30 days.

Niall explained to *The Guardian*, "*Crusher* is a story that I've wanted to write for years. Finally it all came together last November when my wife challenged me to take part in the novel writing event."

Niall was quite happy with the results and, in taking a cue from his wife's fan fiction roots, was all set to self-publish the work. But James suggested that he give the manuscript to their agent, Valerie Hoskins, to read. Valerie ultimately thought enough of the manuscript to pass it along to Random House, which decided to publish it.

Much of the press surrounding *Fifty Shades* had degenerated to being less about the books and more about how people were latching onto the *Fifty Shades* concept for fun and profit.

Hardware stores were reporting an increase in sales of ropes and other forms of BDSM equipment by those interested in wanting to try out the lifestyle. Men's clothing stores were reporting a ten-fold increase in the sales of gray neckties (the closest thing to Christian's silver neck pieces). One hotel made headlines when it reportedly replaced the bible with a copy of *Fifty Shades* in each of its rooms. One airline had reportedly floated the idea of a *Fifty Shades* mile-high club package. *Fifty Shades* spoofs in various media were being proposed.

And no less a publication than *The International Business Times* was widely quoted when they released the news that the Australian women's swim team was relaxing during down time at the London Summer Olympics by reading the *Fifty Shades* books.

Much in the way that *Twilight* had been an economic shot in the arm for the struggling economy of Forks, Washington, James' use of Portland and Seattle as the backdrop for her story was also having that effect in those cities. Locals reported an increase in tourist traffic in and around the locales described in the books and there was some talk that the cities might organize *Fifty Shades* tours of specific locations.

Fifty Shades' impact on the world of classical music was felt into the summer months when a musty old bit of 16th century classical music, Thomas Tallis' "Spem In Alium," was suddenly catapulted to the top of the most downloaded classical singles charts. The reason was that, during a rather powerful bit of BDSM in *Fifty Shades*, Christian reveals that "Spem In Alium" was the music being played in the background during their sexual encounter.

James most certainly took these reports with good humor. After all, imitation was the sincerest form of flattery and, in the case of *Fifty Shades*, it did nothing more than continue to fan the flames of interest in her books. At the end of the day, it was all amusing and all good.

And in their never-ending search for anything *Fifty Shades* to hang a banner headline on, one enterprising journalist from MTV managed to get an audience with *Twilight* author Stephenie Meyer on her opinion of *Fifty Shades* and, more importantly, her response to the ongoing issue of *Fifty Shades* being little more than *Twilight* fan fiction done up for adult consumption.

"I haven't read it (the book)," offered Meyer. "That's really not my genre, my thing. But good for her. She's doing well. That's great. It might not exist in the same form that it's in (without its *Twilight* origins). Obviously James had a story in her, so it would have come out in some other way."

Meyer's seemingly letting James off the hook received mixed notices. Sides had already been chosen on the issue and so, ultimately, nobody's mind seemed changed.

For the rest of the publishing industry, the massive success of *Fifty Shades* had opened the floodgates of a new kind of gold rush and everybody was now looking for their own E L James.

E-books were now serious business and many with the hint of *Fifty Shades* in them were being snapped up by mainstream publishers, a few at seven-figure advances. In one case, an entire e-book publishing company, Authors Solutions, was snapped up by a major house. In a few cases, recently published romance novels had their covers quickly redesigned to reflect a more *Fifty Shades* sensibility.

This was imitation being the sincerest form of flattery at its most money driven. Most likely it would be a double-edged sword. Some authors would be plucked from obscurity and, perhaps for the first time, make considerable money for their efforts. However, the reality was that few if any of these late-in-the-game pick-ups would ever approach the international popularity of *Fifty Shades*.

Not surprisingly, stories began to emerge that writers following in James' path were guaranteed big paydays and celebrity. John Locke, in a *Publishers Weekly* story, was spotlighted as an author who, after going the e-book route and doing quite well, to the tune of a reported million copies sold, was signed to a hard copy distribution deal with major mainstream publisher Simon & Schuster. According to *PW,* the print release of his already successful book managed to sell a mere 6,000 copies by early January 2012 and, according to the story, was not showing the hoped-for success despite a full marketing and publicity campaign. But the story also reported that before the

Fifty Shades feeding frenzy, self-published young adult author Amanda Hocking had caught the attention of St. Martin's Press, which offered her a $2 million, four-book deal on her upcoming series. So the moral of the story was that not every author should count on duplicating E L James' success.

James took the high road in responding to the news that publishers were trying to piggyback on her success. As long as people were buying books and reading, she reasoned, she had no problem with erotica's newfound popularity.

Nor did she have any problems dealing with the incessant questions and speculation regarding the *Fifty Shades* movie. She was accommodating and patient when the subject was broached. And equally good-natured in explaining that the process was moving at the pace that most film deals do. Which meant it was moving very slowly.

But shortly, the next step in the long journey would be taken.

Midway through June, James and her agent Valerie once again hopped a plane for Hollywood. Word was that the search for a producer for *Fifty Shades*, much like the process of the film deal itself, had been narrowed down to a handful of suitors and that Universal and Focus wanted James in town for a final run-through of candidates. James was encouraged by the pitches by some of the top names in the industry and was convinced that whoever was chosen to produce the films would do right by her literary baby.

In the meantime, James had turned her attention to some more real world issues. Namely a new home.

Word leaked out of the London papers and

eventually went viral that James and her husband were actively searching for a larger home. The screaming headlines indicated that the couple had their eye on a particular property, a seven-bedroom mansion not too far from their current home that carried a hefty price tag of 3 million pounds. An extravagant purchase for somebody of relatively modest tastes until one realized that the purchase of film rights would essentially cover that cost.

Not surprisingly the news had supporters and detractors lining up on both sides of this very minor story. Many were of the "you go, girl" school of thought, that she had earned her riches so why not enjoy the ability to move on up. Others prone to petty jealousies derided James for throwing her money around in a very diva-like fashion.

This story triggered yet another round of news items centered around just how much James had made off the books and now movie deal. Most were mere speculation but some actually did a bit of homework; case in point being a Perez Hilton item that indicated that, based on a standard royalty rate, coupled with the proceeds from the movies and merchandising, the author was worth $50 million. The reality was that James had earned more money in a year than she would need in a dozen lifetimes. She would never have to work another day in her life.

And given the nature of pop culture, there was cause to consider that James might just take the money and ride off into the sunset. It would not be the first time an author had written a groundbreaking book and then slipped quietly into obscurity. Does *To Kill A Mockingbird* ring a bell? And despite his best efforts,

J.D. Salinger could not shake the "one and done" reputation that followed *Catcher In The Rye* and eventually retired to obscurity with one classic under his belt and a couple of follow-up books that people have trouble remembering.

But those who knew James knew she was not one to rest on her laurels.

The author was nothing if not loyal to her London roots and had been feeling a bit guilty about concentrating all her book tour appearances in the United States. And so on July 2, she appeared for the first time in front of 450 locals at an interview/book signing event in the hallowed halls of the Institute of Engineering and Technology. The event showcased London readers as every bit as enthusiastic as their U.S. counterparts. This London unveiling was raucous and brash as only a room full of British could be. For James, this event was made all the more successful by the fact that when she would drop a very British term or word, there was no question that the audience would understand her.

And unlike her previous U.S. book tour, the sense of looseness extended to the Q&A portion of the event. The questions and responses seemed less pre-screened and more wide-ranging. Consequently, the audience, and ultimately those who would read the transcript, heard a much more candid James.

James flew back to the States the second week in July because she was going to be a featured guest at the San Diego Comic Con. But those reading between the lines speculated that there was another reason for her being in California.

The reason became clear on July 9 when it was

announced that Michael De Luca and Dana Brunetti would produce the *Fifty Shades* films. The pair brought massive credentials to the table. De Luca's producing credits included the recent Brad Pitt film *Moneyball* and, much earlier, the cult classic *Boogie Nights*. In conjunction with Brunetti, the pair had produced the award-winning *The Social Network* and the latest Tom Hanks vehicle, *Captain Phillips*.

In a prepared statement, James acknowledged her appreciation for the choices and, in particular, her good feelings about De Luca. "I am thrilled that Mike has joined Team *Fifty*," she said. "He brings passion, an in-depth understanding of the characters and the story and a wealth of experience in making quality movies."

James wasted little time in getting down to the nuts and bolts of making the movie with the producers. Not long after the announcement, James met with De Luca and Brunetti for a get-to-know-you dinner in which they exchanged pleasantries and early notions of what the movies should be. The reason this much is known is that Brunetti tweeted about the dinner meeting the next day. James, in the spirit of the moment, followed up with a joking tweet about how she could not find her shoes the next morning.

What was not in the tweets was the particulars, if any, that were discussed. Speculation from industry insiders was that the first course of business would be a script, then a director, then casting. These things take time, especially when, in the case of casting, you are essentially locking actors in for the entire series. Fans who were hoping for a movie relatively soon were resigned to the fact that the first *Fifty Shades* movie would arrive much later.

But that did not stop the Internet universe from running wild with rumors and speculation. A tweet alleging to be from writer Jim Piddock, claiming he had been chosen to write the script, sent fans into a frenzy until Piddock's agents followed with a tweet that it was absolutely not true. In fact the rumors regarding the film were flying so thick and fast that the newly minted producers were faced with having to tweet to set the record straight.

Producer Brunetti was good-natured in debunking the rumors. "All of the rumors on *Fifty Shades* are just that, rumors. No one has been cast in any role. We have to get a writer and director first."

Another question that was most certainly discussed in the early meetings between James and the producers was how graphic *Fifty Shades* was going to be. A segment of the fan base had long speculated that a true film version of the story would have to be rated NC-17. But the reality of the involvement of a mainstream studio and producers pretty much laid that notion to rest.

Still James remained cautiously optimistic and good-natured about the fate of her baby in a Hollywood Life story. "I'm very concerned about how it will play out on screen," she said. "They don't have to do full-on fuckery. This can be done with great taste."

Fifty Shades The Movie would most certainly be an R.

Maybe a hard R?

CHAPTER FIFTEEN
BUY ME, BUY MY UNDERWEAR

Lost in the rush to praise E L James' literary breakthrough is the fact that, at her core, she is a pretty savvy businesswoman who has always seemed to have her eyes on the bottom line.

One could sense that early on when, rather than be a big fish in a financially lacking fan fiction pond, James took the first hint of a groundswell of popularity and fled to the promised land with The Writer's Coffee Shop. Even in those early days, the question of a big payday was never far from her thoughts.

In a Crushable story that chronicled the alleged evidence that once she became famous James turned her back on the fan fiction community, she was quoted in old chat blogs as being very much about the bucks.

"When you publish on Amazon, there's still going to be some negativity (referring to charges from the fan fiction community). But I'm sure it's easier to take with a big fat paycheck."

"I think I've proven that I can write. Now I want to capitalize on it."

Nobody had argued that James did not have the right to get wealthy off her writings. Secretly most writers struggling to make a living at their chosen craft were the biggest and most encouraging supporters of her success. But along the road many felt either she had listened to the wrong people or made some questionable decisions when it came to cashing in.

Exhibit A: The book tour.

There is absolutely nothing wrong with a book tour. Sign some books, glad-hand and schmooze with your fans, pose for pictures. And James did just that. And the so-called events that dotted the tour were fine. But where James and her handlers dropped the ball to many observers was that the three-ring circuses were at a hefty price. Ranging in cost from $20 to $185 to hear an all-too-brief and pre-screened interview/Q&A and drink some cheap wine was cited as a bit exploitive to the fans who had already bought all of James' books. Even the most positive coverage of the tour often referred to the fact that housewives and working women were paying for the privilege.

Where the money was going was never explained. And when James and her people did not respond to the charges, the cynics could only speculate that it was going into somebody's already very full pocket.

What many considered an even bigger betrayal came in mid-June when it was announced that James had finalized a deal with international licensing agent Caroline Mickler to create and merchandise all manner of tie-in items for the assumed impulse buyers who now perceived *Fifty Shades* as an all-consuming lifestyle and passion.

In stories trumpeted by the likes of *The Hollywood Reporter,* the *New York Post* and *Publishers Weekly*, it was noted that the licensing deal would consist of such items as lingerie, sleepwear, perfumes, beauty products, bedding, home furnishings, stationary, jewelry and adult products.

Agent Valerie Hoskins and Mickler were quoted in praising the deal in the most glowing terms. But what was telling in Mickler's quote was the use of the word "brand." To many observers, that statement, as well as the notion of the deal itself, struck many as a code word for "sellout." In all fairness, this was not the first time an author had been turned into a conduit for cheap trinkets. J.K. Rowling, Fay Weldon, Bret Easton Ellis and just about any blockbuster movie with a "based on the best-selling novel" had gone the route of merchandising and tie-in trinkets. James was just proving to be the latest.

And while the mainstream press reported the deal with tongue firmly planted in cheek, smaller-scale websites and blogs, many of whom had championed the author when she was an unknown, were less kind in their assessment of the deal. And the headlines pretty much told it all.

Entertainment And Stars blared, "*Fifty Shades of Grey* Author E L James Turns Fifty Shades Of Greed?"

Screen Crush went for the jugular when it proclaimed, "*Fifty Shades of Grey* Merchandise Gives Us More To Hate."

Into August 2012, James continued to seem more interested in signing merchandising deals than writing. In an announcement carried by the likes of Digital Spy and Gossip Cop, it was announced that James had signed a deal that would allow three different companies to produce and market a line of clothing and underwear inspired by her books. Among the items that would be available were underwear, nightshirts, pajamas, stockings and garter belts.

James proved once again hard to find with a quote regarding the merchandising deal.

To be sure, not every attempt at squeezing blood out of the *Fifty Shades* turnip was being met with such revulsion. The re-release of the three *Fifty Shades* books as a boxed set was meeting with positive feedback and brisk sales to many who already owned the books, as was the announcement that the *Fifty Shades* books would soon be available in hardcover format. And the ongoing saga of the *Fifty Shades* movie continued to thrive on positive and less cynical press who had long ago determined that a movie deal was quite simply part of the process.

But the turn to merchandising had the effect of resurrecting words like "cash cow" and "exploitation." What inevitably happened was that James and her handlers' extracurricular money-making ventures were having the effect in many corners of calling her writing efforts into question.

The fact that she was considering rewriting the *Fifty Shades* storyline from Christian's point of view, once thought of as a way to not only add new perspective but to appease the fans who just could not get enough, had now begun to take on a jaundiced perspective. Why continue to ride the *Fifty Shades* horse when James had made numerous statements that she was working on another non-*Fifty Shades* book? For that matter, enough time had passed for James to have put out something else; even a short story or two would suffice.

There were dire predictions in some corners that James was truly a one-trick pony and that she was jumping on the merchandising bandwagon to cash out rather than to attempt the seemingly impossible task of writing something that would match the popularity of *Fifty Shades*.

E L James was fighting a battle midway through 2012. Was she truly an author capable of great things? Or had she become a brand at the expense of creativity and talent?

The world would watch and wait.

CHAPTER SIXTEEN
THE LIVING IS EASY

Fifty Shades had now officially gone international. Which meant so had E L James.

To help publicize their respective releases, the author had made quick jaunts to Milan, Madrid, a stop in Los Angeles, then back across the pond to Amsterdam. Her frequent flyer miles were rapidly closing in on her book sales. But one thing was certain...July in Los Angeles sure beats the hell out of July in London. James was finding that out firsthand.

Even though the days were primarily filled with business, much of it centering around the announcement of the *Fifty Shades* film producers, James got out often enough to realize what a perfect sunlit day, even with the hint of smog and the occasional early morning overcast, could be.

James had definitely caught the wave of summer in the city, peaceful and laidback with only the occasional meetings, which she found were likewise held in a breezy Hollywood manner. For the moment, James was quite happy to experience the often fairy-tale nature of the Hollywood life firsthand.

There were moments when James was most likely

missing Niall and her children. Business trips had kept them apart on several occasions since late May and, in her private moments, she was almost certainly wishing for the quiet times at home.

But for the moment, she could put those thoughts aside. Because she was going to Comic Con. Thoughts of her previous visit brought a smile to her face. Hanging out with good friends and good drink amid crowds of outrageously costumed fans who truly believed in the power of a fantasy life.

This time around, it would be different. Her last appearance in San Diego had been more of an afterthought. She had just enough notoriety based on her *Master of The Universe* stories to qualify for a slot on a marginally attended fan fiction panel. This time around, she was at the top of the A-list celebrity lineup and people would be lining up around the block to see her.

And there would be no pressure. Because you could not get any bigger than James was right now.

"This has been so hugely surreal," James told the *Los Angeles Times* in response to a question of how she's dealing with the sudden rush of success. "I've had no time to digest it. The first book came out in April (in the U.S.). The next two came out two weeks later. The U.K. followed a week after that. That was April. This is July. We've done a film deal and we've gone into 42 languages. So no, I haven't had time to process this."

Despite the fact that what she did was not considered comic book material, James was considered a perfect fit for Comic Con which, in recent years, had branched off into a multi-media experience that included movies, television and music. And who could argue that the fantasy elements of the *Fifty Shades* books did not reside in the comic book world?

James' schedule at Comic Con turned out to be fairly light. She would not be involved in any panel discussions. She would sign books and do a couple of one-off interviews and that would be it.

James was very much at ease when she arrived at Comic Con on July 12. An estimated 300 tickets had been made available for the signing and had been snapped up instantly by rabid fans. There was excitement in the air. James had quickly climbed the ladder of acceptance in the eyes of comic book devotees. In the best sense of the word, she was now a geek like the rest of them.

Many of James' fans had dressed in comic/fantasy-styled costumes and, as they approached her for a signature and a moment of contact, James found the whole experience surreal in a good way. There was a sense of sincerity that played itself out several times in the signing line.

One woman excitedly told James that she got all the credit for her being pregnant for the third time. A man high-fived James after she had signed his wife's e-reader. And there were reports that several women broke down in tears of thanks for James' books and the message of hope and fulfillment they offered.

Normally leery of large crowds, James put aside her fears during her Comic Con stay and toured the convention floor amid the rush and jostling of thousands of fans. She was readily approachable and made a point of connecting with attendees. At one point she was seen hanging out with a bunch of *Twilight* devotees, perhaps a subconscious nod to her fan fiction roots.

The interviews she did were very informal affairs, with James holding court with a cup of coffee at her side and a muffin in her hand on patios near the convention hall. There was not the pressure there had been when she was the new kid on the block. And she most certainly did not have to do a super selling job on her books, since just about every reader on the planet had long ago tasted the power of *Fifty Shades*. For James, even the serious business of promoting had become just one good time.

The questions asked were the obvious ones. But James did her best to give them a slightly different spin. At night she was the belle of the ball at several Comic Con get-togethers. We know this because James was a literal tweeting machine, enthusiastically letting her family and friends know what she was up to.

After her Comic Con experience, there remained one final bit of public relations to deal with. James traveled to nearby Carlsbad for a book signing at the Costco store. It was a seemingly odd choice for a best-selling author to meet her fans in a bastion of bulk buying. But in a way, it seemed to fit. This is where many of her readers shopped. And James was insistent that it was her duty to embrace her readers where they lived, even if it was in a place that was famous for mammoth boxes of breakfast cereals and condiment jars the size of footballs. Like Comic Con, it was surreal in a whole different way. And surreal was where James wanted to be.

The Carlsbad Patch reported that a line of 1,200 people snaked through the store. They asked the usual questions, were effusive in their praise and thanks. Some cried. Some blushed. According to news reports, at one point, store employees had to cut off the line. Otherwise James might have been there for hours. If she had been, she would have done so willingly.

Costco would be James' last official act. Niall and the boys were flying out to join her for a well-deserved holiday. After a seemingly endless round of professional obligations, the author was looking forward to some quiet time at a location she refused to disclose.

But those who followed James closely were pretty sure they knew what was on her getaway wish list: a month-long stay at a sunny secluded beach. The time to read a good book, something she had not done in a while. And of course her standard response: "To lie down in a small dark room."

During an interview with *UT San Diego*, she acknowledged that she was going on vacation and indicated that, despite her worldwide popularity and that everybody seemed to know what she looked like, she could indeed go away and have some quiet time below the radar of public scrutiny.

"I don't think people really know who I am," she said. "At least I hope not. So I think I can go away and vacation peacefully."

CHAPTER SEVENTEEN
THE MAGIC WORDS

Never say never.

The words have become E L James' mantra when it comes to what she is going to do next. The oft-speculated return to *Fifty Shades* as told from Christian's point of view?

Never say never.

By this time, James had turned the all too often asked question into a bit of sport. Depending on how she felt on a particular day or to what degree she wanted to stir the pot, she would offer just enough to drive the curious mad with speculation. Such as the day when, during an All About You interview, she said, "I'm not sure I would be comfortable writing that. I would like to write something else." But never far from a response was... never say never.

Future projects. Never say never. What she had for breakfast? Well, you get the picture. But into July 2012, it looked like her "magic words" had been a smokescreen

When previously asked about what she was up to, James would dance around the question by saying that she was revisiting a couple of earlier novels but would rarely launch into specifics. Now her legions of fans were finding out that James had been quite the literary worker bee, right under their noses.

In those spare moments when she was not obligated to *Fifty Shades* in some way, James was stealing away to the privacy of her computer and her thoughts.

She finally admitted in a *USA Today* conversation, which was ultimately picked up by numerous websites like Gossip Cop and Vulture, that she does, in fact, already have two other novels completed and in the can; one an erotic story allegedly not related to the *Fifty Shades* universe and the other a young adult paranormal adventure. She seemed excited at the prospect of getting something new and different out but stated that no publication date had been announced for either of these books. While letting people know that there was new and potentially different books on the way, she had made no bones about how her greatest hit is most certainly already behind her.

"I have lots of good ideas but how do you top this (*Fifty Shades*)?" she said. "I've set the bar quite high in terms of storytelling."

As if things could not get rosier, it was announced in late July that total sales for the three *Fifty Shades* books had officially eclipsed the sales of the combined sales of the *Harry Potter* novels to claim the title of all-time paperback best-seller on Amazon.

Broken records and amazing sales had become almost commonplace when it came to *Fifty Shades'* success. One would have thought that James would have become bored by it all. But the author continued to be like a child opening presents on Christmas morning as she responded to this latest milestone.

"How do I feel about that? I'm overwhelmed," she said during an interview at her first U.K. signing event. "I'm completely and utterly overwhelmed by the ridiculous figures that these books seem to be creating. Holy shit! It just boggles my mind."

As did the seemingly endless wheel of promotion that Vintage had her on. In early August it was announced that James would launch a fall U.S. tour that would consist of stops in Houston, Minneapolis, San Francisco and Los Angeles. Of particular interest would be stops in Seattle and Portland, locations that played prominently in the *Fifty Shades* storyline.

However, it was the scheduled stops in Southern California that immediately set tongues to wagging. It was speculated that James would be in Los Angeles to help publicize any announcements of casting and directing decisions for the *Fifty Shades* movie. Like just about everything else in the *Fifty Shades* world, it was merely rumor. But the rumors continued to thrive because nobody was commenting for the record.

Unlike the previous U.S. tour, this would be a scaled-back, book-signing only jaunt without the bells, whistles and circus atmosphere that had accompanied the previous tour. From a business point of view it seemed to make sense; hit all the important major and secondary markets that James missed the first time around. James' level of exhaustion the last time around may have had something to do with a less expansive go round.

But from a promotional sense, more than one person behind the scenes at Vintage obviously thought it was a good idea to keep the buzz going. James had recently celebrated the one-year anniversary of the initial release of *Fifty Shades* and sales continued to skyrocket. But there were most likely backroom concerns, and some scattered news reports, that indicated that sales may have finally reached their peak and were starting to decline. Admittedly the latter news was totally relative because, even with a drop-off, *Fifty Shades* was still selling in the millions. But with no new book on the horizon, it seemed like a win-win to keep James on the road and in front of the press and the public.

It would be another run at being in the limelight and dealing with unbridled adulation. And even at this late day, even with one tour already under her belt, it was still an uneasy cross for James to bear.

"Fame. That's the bit I am uncomfortable with," she conceded to All About You. "It's not something I bargained for at all."

The upside was that James would once again be exploring new places and meeting new people. She was particularly keen on finally being on the ground in the cities that weighed so heavily in the *Fifty Shades* universe. The downside was that she would be leaving her husband and children behind.

James would once again be separated from her family. She acknowledged to an audience during a speaking engagement that her husband, also being a writer, quite understood the realities of promotion and the time she was spending away from home.

"My kids are hilarious. They're completely bemused by all of this as well. They know that I'm not around a lot at the moment. My husband has always worked from home and so he's always done the shopping and cooking. I do the laundry. It's been fine with him."

Of course the tabloids were almost certainly on the hunt for a hint of trouble in paradise for the biggest-selling writer in the world. Scandal sheet veterans had seen more marriages crumble under the weight of celebrity than they could shake a stick at. And the cynics were convinced that it would only be a matter of time before James was added to that list.

But what they discovered was that James was too level-headed to be caught in even a hint of scandal and that, when away from the duties of best-selling author, she had remained a disarmingly normal wife and mother in good standing and an author who had struck literary gold. Those angles had been done to death.

Yes, she did have an actual Red Room in her house. But it was a spare bedroom painted red and the most exciting thing she did in that room was the ironing.

So it seemed that there was nothing new to add.

Consequently, what little news coming out of the *Fifty Shades* camp was sparse and, well, not overly newsworthy. But at its slightest, anything *Fifty Shades* was never less than interesting.

It was only a matter of time before *Fifty Shades* became fodder for daytime and nighttime talk shows. Ellen DeGeneres brought her audience to tears with an attempted straight-faced reading of a *Fifty Shades* passage. Dr. Oz ran with *Fifty Shades* as a jumping off point to what passed for a serious look at sexuality and libido. Wacked-out comic Gilbert Gottfried's video reading had viewers laughing while a *Saturday Night*

Live skit on the whole *Fifty Shades* notion had fans rolling in the aisles.

Observers of the TV approach to *Fifty Shades* were of two minds. Many thought that by the time television got around to exploiting anything, the ride was pretty much over. Others pointed to the fact that James' books were continuing to sell at an amazing clip despite the avalanche of press and had pretty much taken on a life of their own.

A survey captured the media's fancy for a time when it revealed that 44 percent of the women polled would rather read a fictional account of a character's sex life than actively participate in their own. It did not take long for yet another survey that indicated that 56 percent of men had performance concerns after their wives had read the books. And when it was discovered that the paintings of longtime artist friend Jennifer Trouton had made cameo appearances in all three of the *Fifty Shades* books, the amused artist became the subject of media scrutiny for a time. Even the reader who voiced the audio versions of the *Fifty Shades* trilogy, Becca Battoe, was fielding interview requests. Into the depths of fringe *Fifty Shades* coverage came the story of an East Coast printing company that had totaled more than 3,000 tons of paper just to keep up with the printing demands of *Fifty Shades* books.

Of course, amid the flood of good news, there would be the occasional pockets of resistance. A symbolic act of defiance took place late in July when two enterprising Cleveland disc jockeys staged a *Fifty Shades* book burning at a local watering hole. According to reports, an estimated 25 copies of James' books and one Nook were tossed into a bonfire. The disc jockeys would insist that the act was not one of censorship.

Taking a cue from the *Fifty Shades* concept, a company called Clandestine came out with a series of glorified fan fiction takes on classic literature with sexed-up versions of such classics of literature as *Pride and Prejudice* and *Jane Eyre*. The conceit was that now readers of these and other books could actually read the down and dirty scenes that were only hinted at in the original source material. Give Clandestine credit for not indicating that their "Classics Exposed" series was anything more than a mercenary cash grab.

James decided that, since music played such an important part in her writing process and that song titles were sprinkled throughout the trilogy to set time, space and mood, it would be a hoot to create three separate soundtracks to each book. The idea proved a smashing success with her legions of readers embracing the soundtracks (and the obvious inducement to download the songs on iTunes) and adding much-appreciated royalties to a number of appreciative artists.

Of course there remained that little matter of a multimillion-dollar film franchise to consider. Into August 2012, James was constantly on the receiving end of questions about the movie. After yet another query during her London speaking engagement, James acknowledged that she was contractually obligated not to say anything.

"I'm not allowed to discuss the movie at all, which is a real shame. Hopefully, after we get a few things in place, it will start to move on. The actual film is a long way down the line."

But despite James' pronouncements that fans should be patient, the notion of a *Fifty Shades* movie franchise to carry them through the years was too much for many to bear. Mock movie trailers began appearing on the Internet, as did *Fifty Shades* spoofs of various quality. Some enterprising bloggers even went so far as to compose songs around the *Fifty Shades* concept.

Casting speculation continued to run wild. Bret Easton Ellis continued his online campaign to get a gig to the point of sheer annoyance. His persistence would result in his official announcement via Twitter that he had been dropped from the short list of writers under consideration to script the first film.

Mere days after Ellis' announcement, *The Hollywood Reporter* reported that the *Fifty Shades* producers had narrowed their list of potential writers to four. On the surface, they appeared rather odd choices to script *Fifty Shades*.

Dan Fogelman had made his bones in the family film arena with the likes of *Bolt* and *Cars 2*. Veena Sud's credits included such darker offerings as the TV series *The Killing* and was reportedly on board to script the remake of Alfred Hitchcock's *Suspicion*. Karen Croner appeared to know her way around novel to film adaptations with the adaptations of the books *Admission* and *One True Thing*. Kelly Marcel earned credits on the former TV series *Terra Nova* and the upcoming Tom Hanks-Emma Thompson feature *Saving Mr. Banks*.

The response to the announced list of potential scriptwriters left many less than thrilled. Observers of the industry speculated that the writers in the running were on the bland, safe and studio-friendly side rather than an outsider who, they reasoned, should be the one to bring *Fifty Shades* to the screen. Still others offered that the writer's selection was a sign that, like endless number of book to film adaptations, *Fifty Shades* was headed for a chopped and channeled shadow of the source material, perhaps to a PG-13 rating. The studio remained quietly confident in the wake of the attacks by the naysayers.

James had no comment on the choices and appeared content to wait out the final choice, which would assuredly be with her blessing.

But she would shake up all the movie speculation when, in mid-August, she broke her silence when it was reported that she felt that actress Shailene Woodley would make a good Anastasia. The 20-year-old actress, whose previous film was *The Descendants* opposite George Clooney, immediately shot to the forefront of casting choices among the fans who tended to side with the author, who put aside the long-standing notion that the film actors for *Fifty Shades* would most likely be total unknowns.

In perhaps the most sincere form of flattery James could get, fan fiction writers began creating and publishing their own fan fiction homages to *Fifty Shades*.

It was something that James could readily understand and, emotionally, she saw it as a true return to her roots.

However, at several events on her book tour, James would be candid in assessing her feelings about fan fiction versions of *Fifty Shades*. She conceded that she had not read any of it and had no plans to. For her it was a defensive measure. She did not want anybody else's notions of her work in her head if she went on to explore the *Fifty Shades* world.

James continued to have the Midas Touch through the summer. Word had quickly gone viral on the author's "soundtrack playlists," which had started as a playful blog entry on her website. Obviously the commercial world was looking for yet another way for *Fifty Shades* to get at readers' wallets and so, in August, it was announced that EMI would release an album of classical music, selected by James and inspired by the books and featuring a *Fifty Shades* book cover as the album cover. The album went digital on August 15 and was released on CD on September 18.

EMI was thrilled at the idea of becoming a, hopefully, profitable appendage of the *Fifty Shades* universe. But that did not stop label spokesperson Wendy Ong from scratching her head at the notion. "Who would have thought classical music and *Fifty Shades of Grey*," she marveled in a conversation with *The Vancouver Sun*. "You know it's a stretch."

Admittedly an album of all classical music was less crass and more legitimate than other *Fifty Shades* cash-in projects and, in a statement, James hinted as much.

"I'm thrilled that the classical pieces that inspired me while I wrote *Fifty Shades* are being brought together in one collection for all the lovers of the books to enjoy."

Not surprisingly the album would go to the top of the charts and, along the way, receive its fair share of even-handed reviews, praising the blatantly commercial venture for bringing classical music to the masses.

In many quarters, the album was viewed as a calculating step in the direction of casting an even wider shadow for the *Fifty Shades* brand. James had already taken the step of creating, allegedly for the fun of it, three long playlists for her three books. Whether by design or circumstance, James, and by association EMI or whoever picked up the music baton, was ensured of a long-running series of albums that would guarantee profits for all involved.

As well as introduce a new generation to the joys of timeless music.

James continued at a leisurely pace through August. Along with millions around the world, she spent much time in front of her television, cheering on the London Olympics and tweeting away her support for both the Irish and Jamaica teams. But by the end of the month, her itinerary was set in stone, her passport was out and she was once again making plans to return to the States and the untold number of fans who lived and breathed her work.

And as always, for James the adulation and the magic of her success most certainly remained unbelievable.

It is impossible to get inside somebody's head. But one can speculate what E L James was thinking and feeling about it all midway through 2012.

A hobby had turned into fame, fortune and had made her the literary torchbearer for women to come out and embrace their fantasies and desires. At this point, it was a ride with seemingly no end in sight.

But if ever a rise from literal unknown to

megastar needed any further validation, it came with the announcement that James had made *Time* magazine's annual list of The 100 Most Influential People In The World.

Years previous, James, in a moment of good-natured bravado, had confided in a friend that her goal was to be interviewed by *Time* as well as to become a publishing sensation.

For E L James, it had all come to pass.

CHAPTER EIGHTEEN
WATCHING AND WAITING

James had no plans for Christmas. Except for a lot of family time and a lot of rest. She would laughingly acknowledge in several interviews and in *The Hollywood Reporter* in particular that she had not slept a wink since January 2012, and freely admitted that she was willingly partaking of and thoroughly enjoying the perks and requirements of her sudden celebrity. Going into 2013, it was now pretty much wait and see as she observed the machinations of Hollywood and the process of turning her erotic trilogy into, hopefully, Hollywood gold.

Despite an extensive background in production at the BBC, James had been a literal babe in the woods during the US film negotiations for *Fifty Shades of Grey* and had trusted the decision made by her executive producers regarding the choice of director and screenwriters. She was certainly given the opportunity to rubber stamp those decisions but that seemed more of a courtesy by the production company than an actual power move, although the author would occasionally concede that having big-time filmmakers come to her for her okay was a bit of a hoot.

And when it came to the lingering and often rumor-filled notices of casting the two leads, James was right there with the fans with equal parts anxiousness and speculation throughout the year. Consequently when it was announced that Dakota Johnson and Charlie Hunnam had been selected midway through 2013, nobody was more relieved than James.

The author told *Entertainment Weekly* that Johnson "was an old soul and she has a wicked sense of humor." And she was quick on Twitter to happily announce that Hunnam was the one for her. "The talented and gorgeous Charlie Hunnam will play Christian Grey in 50 Shades of Grey," she had tweeted.

Less than a month after the casting announcement, James would be forced to eat her words when Hunnam unexpectedly left the film, alternately sighting scheduling conflicts with his day job, the television series *Sons of Anarchy*, and a disagreement with the direction of his character and the script. Always upfront with her readers and, by association, the fan base for the film, James once again tweeted her reaction in a quote that appeared in *Entertainment Weekly*. "It was disappointing news. But it is what it is."

James was not one to back off from the controversy surrounding Hunnam's unexpected exit and once the dark cloud had settled, the studio rushed to find a worthy replacement for her beloved Christian. Along with the Universal Studio chairman, the Fifty Shades' producers and the director, James produced a list of four male actors she felt would be worthy replacements.

While the lists of proposed names were never released, it was most certainly James' very British ways and attitudes that were instrumental in bringing two UK television actors, Jamie Dornan and Christian Cooke, back from their previous elimination in the first round of auditions that had produced Hunnam, to prime target status for another chance. Ultimately it would be Dornan who would step in to play Christian.

But months before the official announcement and the ensuing drama, James was never far from the whirlwind of Fifty Shades that constantly stalked her.

Running a close second to the speculation regarding the film was the continued questions regarding a next book. Die-hard fans were hoping against hope for a continuation of the Fifty Shades saga. Others were simply anxious for another James book period. Early in 2013 James dropped a statement in answer to those those questions when she stated to *The Guardian* that "I'm looking forward to bringing you some new love stories that I've got planned. I never say never to more Fifty Shades stories, but for now they are on the backburner. But I have other stories to tell first."

In the wake of all this speculation even the hint of a new book was made headline. The press dredged up a 2012 impromptu interview with a Vintage book rep during a James book signing in which the rep indicated that a fourth Fifty Shades book was actually completed and that he had read the first five pages of the manuscript on a computer. Not many took his comments seriously.

Around the same time, *The Independent* came calling, asking James if it was true that her contract with Vintage indicated that she owed the publisher three more books. Her response was simply, "I'm under no pressure. I do it [writing] for fun. I wouldn't do it otherwise."

There was an element of defiance in James' remarks. Defiance that many speculated was in response to pressure, perhaps equal parts from her publisher and her fans, that she should be writing something new at this point.

But while James insisted there was another book on the horizon, Tish Beaty, her editor on the first Fifty Shades book and currently a literary agent, indicated in a 2014 interview with this author that it might be all talk and a lot of pressure that was driving James' current pronouncements.

"She may be feeling the pressure," said Beaty. "I'm sure she's getting pressure from her fans and the literary community, as well as her publisher. There's the pressure of proving that she's not a one-hit wonder and that she can write something other than fan fiction. It could go either way. She could have another book ready or she might well be waiting until after the movie comes out."

Or it could be that James, not unlike author Harper Lee who only had *To Kill A Mocking Bird* in her and never wrote another book again, had only the three volumes of Fifty Shades in her and the creative tank is totally on empty.

"It's a possibility," said Beaty. "*Fifty Shades* came at a time when fan fiction was really hot. There was a lot of inspiration and a big fan base. It was a very different atmosphere than it is now. When you have a publisher waiting on you, that's a whole different pressure. It could be that it's all become too much for her."

In the meantime, James was taking every opportunity for some quiet time with her family. Her husband Niall, who continued to enjoy his own bit of literary success, albeit on a much lower, below the radar level with his novel *Crusher*, remained the loyal and loving husband whose own expertise in the film world was a constant reminder to James about the reality of the film business.

James' by now two teenaged-sons were used to their mother's frequent business trips and the inherent celebrity and media interest and were basically taking it all in stride. "They are incredibly proud of me," she told *USA Today*. "They are bemused at it. They make fun of me, which is completely natural."

And what James was discovering during her time away from public scrutiny was how those who lived around her had learned to cope with their celebrity neighbor. Early on, the curiosity factor would consistently result in neighbors approaching her on the street and accosting her with questions and autograph requests. And not too far behind were the journalists who, when they couldn't get a word with James, would question the neighbors for even the slightest tidbits. But these days the neighbors were rarely bothered and most exchanges between James and her neighbors were quick, informal and matter of fact.

Like they used to be.

James continued to bask in the celebrity limelight, doing the occasional interview and attending more Hollywood-type parties. It was at one such event, the A ticket Vanity Fair Oscar party, that she hinted that she might, in fact, have another book ready to hit the shelves. James' follow up to the Fifty Shades' trilogy had long been speculated upon but, beyond the never-ending rumors of three additional books telling the Fifty Shades' story from Christian's point of view and a vague reference to a young adult paranormal romance, many were concerned that James had truly taken the money and ran and that there would never be another book.

Beaty is not surprised that James has gravitated toward the celebrity side of what she has accomplished. "I think she's become her own little star. She's very much in the spotlight and she's pretty much propelled herself into the spotlight. James has been very hands-on in cultivating the adulation and popularity; the merchandising, the sex toys. She's on top of everything. James knows what she's doing when it comes to that kind of thing."

Beaty speculated that having her hands in so many of the ancillary offshoots of her books, as well as the enormous amounts of money those things generate, may well be the cause of what many impatient observers feel is her writer's block in which much is promised but, as of yet, nothing is delivered.

"Financially she's set for life," said Beaty. "But there are a lot of writers set for life who they just do it because they love it."

At the ultra-chic Vanity Fair Party, James teased to *The New York Post* that "My next book won't be nearly so raunchy and I will probably write it under another name."

Meanwhile the bottom line types at her publisher Vintage Books were secretly hoping that there was some reality to their best-selling author's pronouncements. While the Fifty Shades books were continuing to sell at amazing numbers, the publisher's collective thinking was that it was time to get another book out of James. They were not about to rush her. But they did have their fingers crossed that another James tome would drop in short order.

"With the movie coming out and the ongoing popularity of everything Fifty Shades, people in the publishing industry want a piece of that," reflected Beaty. "James is still on the rise as an author. Ideally the next six months to a year would be the time for her to come out with another book."

Finally the creative log jam was broken in March when Vintage Books announced a collaboration between James and Vintage for what was essentially a hybrid writer's guide/journal consisting of snippets of advice from James and a number of blank pages for readers to jot down their own thoughts. *Fifty Shades of Grey: Inner Goddess (A Journal)* was released on May 1 and was an immediate disaster.

Many saw the notion as a cruel joke given the ongoing question of the quality of how good a James' writing. And there was no getting away from the gimmicky/stop gap idea of throwing something out on the tiles to keep the fans primed for the next novel. The result was that *Fifty Shades of Grey: Inner Goddess (A Journal)* sold poorly and many of those who bought it were quick to hit the internet to share their disappointment of it all. Ultimately it was a poor business decision that most certainly hurt James' credibility.

Suddenly the conjecture that James had hit major

writer's block or, even more telling, that the failure to follow up the Fifty Shades books with anything new meant that James, quite satisfied with the nearly $100 million she was set to earn during the year, much of which was derived from film and merchandising rights, had sent her into an early retirement. There continued to be hints of other books already completed or planned but, with nothing forthcoming, even James' most ardent supporters were having their doubts.

Beaty speculated that James might be emotionally overwhelmed with all her success and might well be having trouble morphing back into a writing mood. "I just don't know when she's had time to write. She's got a big following. She could put out crap and people would buy it. I'm interested in her future. I would like to see something else. A lot of people liked what she wrote in the past and the way she just hammered it out. It didn't seem too difficult for her. Most authors have a process. They have somewhere they can go to write. At some point she may just have to reign all the other things in, go away and just do it."

James seemed impervious to any backlash caused by the *Inner Goddess* journal fiasco, continuing to hopscotch back and forth between the UK and the US and, by June 2013, becoming a regular A list presence at many Hollywood get-togethers. She was a special guest invitee at a birthday party thrown by Robert Pattinson for a friend where James mixed and mingled easily and answered the inevitable Fifty Shades rumors and speculations. During one allegedly drunken moment with screenwriter/gadfly Brett Easton Ellis, she reportedly stated that Pattinson was her first choice to play Christian Grey.

But as it would turn out, James had not completely left her roots behind for the Hollywood high life. In early May, both Smart Bitches/Trashy Books.com and Before The News.com reported that James, reportedly under a covert bit of secrecy that included wearing a name tag with a fake name on it, attended the annual *Romantic Times* convention in the states. But she blew her own cover from the audience of a panel discussion when she rose to personally correct a false statement about her publishing history.

Needless to say, once James' cover was blown, the Twitterverse went electric with reports that instantly contradicted each other. Many felt that James' appearance had cast a destructive pale on the proceedings; acknowledging that she would not do interviews and that she had admonished those within earshot to not talk about her books. Others countered that the author had actually been quite cordial and had done her best to blend in with the crowd. Obviously an impossible task.

Her summer jaunt in America continued apace with a return for the San Diego Comic Con. James relished this return trip as her initial foray into pop culture heaven had been both a joyous and relatively easy replay of the level of fandom that had garnered her the earliest success. Her second Comic Con would be very much the same with the added element of this time having the movie version of Fifty Shades to promote. As always, James gravitated toward the legitimate innocence and excitement of the comic book crowd. The questions were the obvious ones for the most part and the crowd took it well when, for whatever reason, she could not or would not answer them.

Midway through 2013, the casting drama was finally out of the way. Relative unknown Jamie Dornan would prove to be a worthy assessor to the Christian Grey throne according to James. As James would tweet the day of the announcement, "Stow your twitchy palms, ladies. Our man is here."

After some back and forth regarding the release date and a spate of new rumors including one that had the production company shooting all three movies in the trilogy back to back and the more tantalizing reveal that the Fifty Shades of Grey movie would be released in both NC-17 and R rated versions, a definite start date for the first movie was announced for November.

James, in the spirit of supporting the film in any way possible, became more amenable to doing press. For the most part the interviews she would do were fairly softball in nature with the predictable questions that she responded to either by not answering them or giving what had by now become pat and predictable answers.

However in an interview with E, there was a sudden sense of vulnerability in her facing the true testament of her rise to celebrity. She came across as quite overwhelmed and believably frightened at the prospect of her baby finally going to the big screen. And for a brief moment E.L. James had disappeared and Erika was once again leading with her emotions.

"I'm completely terrified," she confessed to the E reporter at the prospect of watching from the sidelines as the movie was made. "My mother was terrified of everything and so was I. It's a terrible way to grow up. You just don't expect the kind of overwhelming success that I'm having."

And she was quick to point out in the E interview

that fandom, to which she was eternally grateful and loyal, was also causing her sleepless nights. "If the movie is bad, they'll blame me. Of course they will. They hold me responsible for everything."

The E interview provided an insight of sorts into the way James was now dealing with the press. Being new to the media game, James, early on, had been reluctant to part with even a hint of personal information, lest it compromise the sense of privacy and normalcy she was trying to maintain. James had been so rigid in this stance that when, in an early radio interview, she inadvertently revealed that her sons attended private school, she called up the radio station post interview and literally demanded that the station edit out the section where she spilled the secret.

However these days James was now more likely to reveal personal tidbits than any information on her books. A case in point being an interview with *The Guardian* in which she casually tossed off, "When I was two and a half, I nearly died of double pneumonia. The earliest memory I had as a toddler was being in an oxygen tent."

Fifty Shades of Grey began production in Vancouver, Canada midway through November. And it was never a question that James would be welcome to come to the set and observe. Book authors on a film set has always been a conceit heavy with potential problems. Consequently it had long been a time honored suggestion, or perhaps a long held Hollywood superstition, that the author might be better suited by staying away. But the producers and filmmakers felt confident enough that everybody was on the same page that James was most certainly welcome.

Excitement built to a fever pitch as James winged her way to Vancouver. She was at once the creator of it all, as well as a curious and anxious fan. How she would react to seeing her characters come to life was anybody's guess.

Finally she was cautiously optimistic that the movie version of *Fifty Shades of Grey* would ultimately reflect her book. "I've had some healthy debates with the filmmakers. It's been interesting."

According to several media reports, James' visits to the Fifty Shades set were nothing short of a love fest. With her down to earth nature and old world charm, James became an immediate favorite of the cast and crew, snapping selfies and spreading good cheer. The already established rapport with director Sam Taylor Johnson was even more pronounced as they were often spotted laughing easily together between filming sessions.

And so it was more than a bit surprising when a report by E indicated that there had been a fallout between author and director over the direction of the script that had turned into a full blown feud with the inevitable 'unnamed sources' indicating that the pair were literally at each other's throats and that James was particularly incensed that the film was taking major liberties with her book. And, in particular, James was allegedly upset with the fact that her sex scenes were not being filmed as they had been described in her books.

On set tabloid-type stories were not uncommon in gossip wild Hollywood press. But James was still new to the game and once everybody connected to the film laughed the reports off, James took a humorous selfie from the set with director Johnson and herself standing together, their faces in mock defiance, raising clenched fists.

It was James' way of declaring to the world that it was all rubbish.

CHAPTER NINETEEN
COUNTDOWN TO FIFTY SHADES

Fifty Shades of Grey filmed its final scenes on February 23, 2014. And shortly after officially wrapping the movie, James was one of the first to break the news to the world. The author tweeted a picture of director Johnson and herself, all smiles and looking a bit dazed. The caption with the photo said, "One of us is drinking. It's a wrap."

However by the time principal photography concluded, what would be a year-long publicity purge racing toward the Valentine's Day 2015 release of *Fifty Shades of Grey* had already fired its first salvo. Midway through January, the first promotional poster trumpeting the film's future release went public and it was an immediate hit. To wit, a very nattily dressed Christian Grey, with his back facing front, is seen looking out the window of his high-rise office and contemplating the sprawling signature Seattle skyline. Underneath the image are the words, 'Mr. Grey Will See You Now."

James and the rest of the world suddenly had a hint of what was to come and they were excited all over again.

Early in February a new secret would be revealed when the man who claimed he was James' inspiration for Christian Grey stepped forward. Alessandro Proto was a quiet, conservative middle-aged Italian real estate agent. Proto, who was found guilty of stock manipulation, coincidentally on Valentine's Day 2013, said in an interview with *The New York Daily News*, that he'd spent two days with James in 2010 in Italy when the soon-to-be author was researching a story about celebrities who were buying up property in Italy.

"Grey's firm is Grey Enterprise Holding," Proto told *The New York Daily News*. "Mine is called Proto Organization Holding. When I met E.L. James, I used to drive an R8 Audi. Christian Grey drives an Audi R8 and he also buys Anastasia an Audi R3."

Proto also explained that his aversion to reporters was also a trait transplanted to Christian Grey. He also noticed that Christian's top floor office suite read a lot like his 8th floor office suite on the top of his building.

But the businessman laughingly acknowledged that Christian' sexual proclivities were definitely not borrowed from him. "Everything that has to do with S&M is pure imagination. I am an old- fashioned man when it comes to sex. I'm not into that kind of fantasy."

Proto made a good case for him being the model for Christian Grey and when James did not respond to Proto's statements, many observers of all things Fifty Shades were convinced they had found their Christian.

With the onset of summer, the growing hype of the movie and James being all too willing to get out and meet her fans, the author made a quick hop back to the states to appear at the Romantic Times Book

Lovers Convention. In upcoming weeks she would also do a long anticipated return to London for another speaking engagement and book signing.

In both instances, James showed that the previous year's round of personal appearances had molded her into a personable and entertaining speaker. Of course it did not hurt that the sheer mania of her appearances overcame the fact that the speeches and subsequent book signings had become predictable. Because truth be known, everything EL James had to say had pretty much been told endless times over. There were the truly tired anecdotes about how she came to write *Fifty Shades*, her background and the largely evasive or vague responses to questions regarding the upcoming movie that bordered more on PR hype than substantive anecdotes. But for James, it was ultimately about reconnecting with the fans, the people who had brought her to this celebrity.

These days, whenever she gave a lecture or did an interview, the question of the next book became an even hotter topic after the failure and the cynical vibe of her *Inner Goddess* journal. Her vague promises to those questions only fueled speculation that James had truly hit a writing wall and that there was not truly a completed next novel in the pipeline. By August, even the excitement generated by the upcoming movie could not completely quell the concerns that, over the past year and a half, James had done a lot of promotion but not much writing.

But she was not alone in that area. Into June and July, the Fifty Shades of Grey publicity push was now officially in high gear. The film's stars Dakota Johnson and Jamie Dornan were doing a seemingly endless round of television, newspaper and magazine interviews. But it would remain for the release of the very first promotional trailer late in July to set the tone for the months to come. Alternately tension-packed and erotic, finally with just a hint of the erotic bits to come, the trailer, backed by Beyoncé's *Crazy In Love*, was an international sensation. James was ecstatic at what she saw and was now fully convinced that the film would do right by her book.

And by August, James must have sensed, that amid the rush of film news, her fans were getting a bit anxious about a new book. Because early in the month the twitterverse was apoplectic with the report, in *The Independent* and elsewhere, that James had posted an Instagram photo of her keyboard that, to the fanatically inclined, appeared to focus on the keys F, I, T, Y. While nothing in the missive indicated the photo was the sign of a forthcoming book, those who seemingly lived and died by Fifty Shades of Grey swore up and down that it meant a new book was coming soon. As always, it was all smoke, mirrors and the power of suggestion at its finest. And, as always, there was nothing definite.

Even more vague bordering on downright delusional was an August tabloid explosion that roared out the news that everybody's favorite train wreck, actress Lindsay Lohan, has indicated that, despite not having a publishing deal in place, she is ready to write her sizzling tell-all autobiography and that she would like James to be her ghostwriter. Obviously it does not take much for the terminally-not- right-in-the-head to select one of the most famous writers to do grunt ghostwriting work. In this case it was James having a brief but reportedly pleasant encounter with Lohan at the Chiltern Firehouse to get the troubled actresses literary juices flowing. James wisely had no comment. And went back to the business of being a big-time writer.

However much time James may or may not be spending doing any actual writing, she most certainly had time to oversee her ever-expanding brand. Early in August, James journeyed to nearby Bath for a meeting with Lovehoney, the adult sex toy retailer who had been marshalling its forces to co-create and co-design with the author, behind a series of bedroom items inspired by the sex toys depicted in her books.

The first run of Fifty Shades sex toys, including restraints, handcuffs, spanking paddles, riding crops and floggers, had been a worldwide success and had, reportedly, accounted for a good part of James' millions. On this day, James and the Lovehoney honchos were being very business-like as they discussed the particulars of a follow-up line of personal vibrators.

But not content to merely talk business, James, at one point, went down to the warehouse and unexpectedly got elbow deep in her products when she joined the workers in packaging the latest orders going out to anxious customers and, in one instance, penned a personal note and dropped it in a box indicating that the person's order had been packaged by E.L. James. In a *Daily Mail* report James stated that, "I'm so excited that the toys that I described in the books have come to life and can be enjoyed around the world."

James had obviously taken a liking to the merchandising side of things and that was most evident when she became involved in the creation and marketing of 50 Shades men's underwear. The form-fitting undergarments had the author's seal of approval and, according to *Metro*, she worked very closely with the photographer and a Jamie Dornan look-alike model in filming the ads for the marketing campaign.

As the Fifty Shades of Grey film juggernaut continued unabated, bits and pieces of news continued to bubble to the surface. It was revealed by Digital Spy in late summer that the Fifty Shades of Grey film franchise was, at one point, being talked about as a possible television series through the persistence of Starz CEO Chris Albrecht who had approached Universal, asking for the rights to the E.L. James novels for a three-season series with each season focusing on one book. His approach hinged on the fact that the books could be done on cable television at a cost-effective budget and that the studio would not have to bank its fortunes on a big theatrical box office. "I'm the guy who called up Universal," said Albrecht, "and told them I would get you all three years on the air as a series." However Universal was looking at the big picture and passed.

It had been a given that the Fifty Shades of Grey film would be the 800 pound gorilla on Valentine's Day 2015 and so it did not appear that the major studios would be putting big films up against it that weekend. But by the end of August it was announced in *The Daily Mail* that a Christian production company was, indeed, going to play David to Fifty Shades' perceived Goliath by opening a much different kind of romantic film on the same weekend. Entitled *Old Fashioned*, the film projects a faith-based storyline in which a young couple meet and fall in love in a chaste relationship, very much in keeping with Christian doctrine.

Old Fashioned's director Rik Swartzweider told *The Daily Mail* that he had no illusions about going up against Fifty Shades but acknowledged that there was definitely a growing market for faith- based films. "This is definitely a David verses Goliath situation. They will have more screens, more money and more hype."

For her part, James was diplomatic when questioned about this cinematic upstart, stating that there was room enough for every film. It's easy to be diplomatic when you're Hollywood's top dog.

Well into September, James continued to enjoy the celebrity perks of being a celebrity in her own life. With the ever-tolerant Niall on her arm, James was the belle of the ball at the GQ Men of the Year awards ceremony in London where she mixed easily with Jamie Dornan and other male tastemakers in the worlds of modeling and acting. There would be a small bit of intrigue during the ceremony and after party. The notorious Lindsay Lohan was in attendance and Jamie had become Fifty Shades notorious when his name had appeared on the troubled actress' sex list. Fortunately for the sake of decorum, both parties kept a respectable distance from each other and no scenes were reported.

James was highly visible on the party circuit during London's Fashion Week, enjoying the non-stop bashes at all the exclusive locals. Of particular note at one toney get-together where one of the other revelers was London's notorious US transplant,

Lindsay Lohan. Selfies circulated showing James in a mask reminiscent of the one displayed on her Fifty Shades book cover while Lohan was all smiles and leggy in black lace. The press had a field day with the meeting, postulating that Lohan, who was never shy about mixing business with pleasure, had actually been trying to convince James to use her influence to get her a role in the second Fifty Shades of Grey film.

Early October brought the inevitable speculation that James was back to writing when Showbiz411 reported that the author was hard at work creating new characters for a non-Fifty Shades book. The tidbits offered in the report indicated the new tome would be a romance but that bondage would figure into the narrative. Those hoping for a quick James fix were no doubt disappointed that this proposed new book would not appear until sometime in 2016, or even later. The story did indicate that along with this new volume, James continued to hint at both a fourth Fifty Shades book as well as a prequel focusing on Christian Grey's life before Fifty.

Midway through October, James' day-to-day activities became less public. She was spending a lot less time in the public eye, if the lack of any new media coverage was any indication, and, most certainly basking in the excitement and hype surrounding the premiere of *Fifty Shades of Grey*, which was now a little more than four months away.

There was no comment to be found when the production company called some last minute reshoots in Vancouver, although the speculation was that James had seen an early cut of the film and had decided certain sections of the film were too thin and that additional scenes were needed to fill the story out. Nor was there a hint of excitement or expectation from the author when it was announced that ticket orders for the premiere Los Angeles showings of the movie were already being taken.

Over the course of years, James had become quite savvy with Internet technology and had always been quick on the twitter finger and often quite opinionated. In later October, one actor, as reported by *Variety*, revealed that the author had cut him to the quick around the time actors were being considered for the role of Christian Grey. Eddie Redmaine, who starred in the film version of *Les Miserables* and *Jupiter Ascending*, was asked during an interview if he were interested in playing the kinky billionaire. He said he was interested. When James got wind of that, she immediately went online and tweeted "under no circumstance." Redmaine got wind of her put-down and responded "Alright, am I that bad? I can put a whip in my hand. I can get all kinky."

James was nowhere to be found for a response.

CHAPTER TWENTY
THE CURTAIN RISES

The publishers of *Fifty Shades of Grey*, ever on the lookout for a way to maximize profits, were taking a traditional approach with the titular title when they announced a new, movie tie-in version of the book featuring a hot and heavy photo from the film would be released in January 2015. From a pure collectors' point of view, it seemed like a good bet as movie tie-ins have a history of lower print runs, inevitably making the edition more valuable for completists.

James was tweeting and texting away about this new version of the book that started it all. But, in the process of doing so, reignited the frustration that, after many proclamations, no new book by the author was in the pipeline. The best the press could muster on the subject was the speculation that James might be planning a surprise of a literary kind shortly after the release of the Fifty Shades of Grey movie, all of which did little to placate the growing cynicism among ardent supporters that there would never be another James book of any sort.

It was first hint of a publishing tie-in to the film and, for James, another anticipatory tingle that the movie would most certainly be a monster success. With the movie well on the way to release, James had been able to put a certain line of questioning behind her. She had answered to death questions regarding what sex scenes had made the movie and how a condensed version of her very deep and dense novel would play. Dakota Johnson? Jamie Dornan? Sam Taylor Johnson? Yes, they were all wonderful and everything connected to the film was just peachy. How many times could she say the same things over and over?

But she knew her work on the movie was far from over. By late November she was already being approached by the film's publicity department with a litany of interviews and press screenings that she just had to participate in. James' answer was to be a good soldier and to trudge on. She was seeing everything Fifty Shades of Grey in her dreams. It was not good for getting a good night's sleep but it was wonderful for her mental well-being with the notion that millions of people were, doubtless, losing sleep over her creation as well.

In late November, *The Sunday Times* did a detailed piece on James's comings and goings in the past year and how immense wealth, reportedly to the tune of $1 million a week, had or had not changed her. The piece was breathless in describing how James still had her hair blow dried in a local shop and did her own supermarket shopping. On the high-end side it reported that James had begun collecting art (specifically artist Peter Blake) and had made approximately forty trips back and forth across the Atlantic for both business and pleasure. Of the latter, three days of partying in Los Angeles were considered a highlight for the author. The piece painted a not too subtle picture of extravagance but James, as reported in *The Sunday Times*, defended herself against the notion that she was now a total material woman.

"I like nice things," she said, "but ever since I've had money, I actually find shopping a lot less pleasurable."

Two years ago that most likely would have sufficed. But by 2014 much of the image that James projects to the world is predicated on the massive amounts she makes and reportedly spends. In an interview with *The Guardian* one could almost sense the sigh and the rolling of her eyes as she once again dealt with the perception of her material side. "I've had the odd moment where I've thought I could buy that. But I've always decided not to in the end. It's just stuff and I've got enough stuff."

She was also reportedly wistful in *The Guardian* piece about taking great pains, despite her worldwide notoriety, to always try to stay in the shadows. "I don't do much press. I value my anonymity."

But as 2014 was rapidly coming to a conclusion, James was being forced to once again step into the spotlight. The success or failure of Fifty Shades of Grey had long hinged on what she felt about the movie. She had been front and center during the making of the movie as a supportive and vocal fan. Now with the movie only two months away from meeting the world, she knew that, shortly, she would once again be stepping out to make happy talk.

It would remain for her to see the completed film for the first time to determine whether James would be telling the truth or blowing smoke.

Early in December it was announced that the official unveiling of Fifty Shades of Grey would take place February 9, 2015 at an undisclosed location in Los Angeles. The gala premiere would be attended by the cast and, according to the announcement, would feature a lavish after-party.

For James, the announcement was once again a time of excitement and nervousness. She was well-aware that director Johnson had been working 24/7 to re-edit the film incorporating the newer material shot in October. Beyond that, she knew as much as the rest of the world.

Which was not much.

Christmas was looming in the James household as a time of happiness and reflection. It would be a pivotal point in James' life and career. She had risen from total obscurity and had been brave enough to run with an idea and her imagination to a level of success that most can only dream of. She had emerged very rich and with her old-fashioned integrity intact. But would New Years be the end of the adventure or the beginning of the next chapter?

As the clock struck midnight James, nestled in the bosom of her family and experiencing life spun out of a dream and into an unbelievable reality, could only look back on what *Fifty Shades of Grey* had brought to her life and ask the same question we are all asking.

What's next?

EPILOGUE
WHEN ALL IS SAID AND DONE

So there you have it. Your classic rags to riches story. Out of obscurity and into the fire. It all happened so fast. It seemed like only yesterday. You haven't missed a thing. You've got it all. E L James is quite literally a by-product of a moment caught in time.

She has come out of nowhere to lay waste to the popular literary landscape. Yes, it is truly an amazing feat done in supernova speed. And to this point it is truly the whole story.

Just how interesting is E L James? In a very down-home, perfectly normal middle-aged wife and mother with an itch to scratch kind of way? Very interesting. She is one of those beacons in the night, inspiring everybody who has dreamed of writing, to work alone into the night. Because now they know they have a chance.

But at the end of the day, the ascendency of *Fifty Shades* and E L James is just the latest piece in an ongoing literary odyssey, a trip up the trail of popular literature, pop culture and the continuing power of the written word to strike sparks like a modern-day flint.

Stephenie Meyer and J.K. Rowling had already carved out the template. Come from out of nowhere with one brilliant idea, turn it into a best-seller and make millions. Only the names, the stories and their lives are different. At the end of the day, they all made it.

Then what?

Meyer and Rowling lowered their profile considerably. Reportedly continuing to write, living the good life off of well-deserved royalties and film money and gearing up for the next stage of their writing life while, suddenly, so far below the radar as to defy the fact that they ever existed in the first place.

This is the reality of the writing life. Nothing to fear here. These authors will be back and so, most certainly, will E L James. But you'll just have to be patient.

We all know that James has at least two more novels tucked away in a drawer somewhere. And while we've been bombarded with the notion that the author will, at some point, rewrite *Fifty Shades* from Christian's viewpoint to feed the habit of legions of fans, don't be surprised or disappointed if the next offering from the world's currently most popular author is light years away from what got her here in the first place.

Imaginations work in strange ways and so it is not out of the realm of possibility that James' dreams have gone off in a highly divergent direction.

It had been any ongoing bit of Q&A business that James' sons had not read any of her books and that the closest they had come to turning a page on *Fifty Shades* was showing their mother where their Latin teacher wanted her copy signed. Maybe the next book would be fit for consumption by teenage boys.

Despite rumors to the contrary, authors are human. They crave the quiet time with loved ones as well as the attention, away from creative chores and obligations. Granted such vacations are generally short-lived. So one should not be too surprised if James, even while sipping a tall cold one on a secluded beach and enjoying the quiet and solitude with her family, is mentally stringing together a tale that might well make *Fifty Shades* pale by comparison.

If you are a true fan of E L James and *Fifty Shades*, you have a lot on your plate. There is much to consider.

And that includes the very smart business sense that James has exhibited when it comes to her literary baby. She knows she has become a brand; that just about anything with a *Fifty Shades* logo on it, at least for the short term, will sell. We may not agree with much of her approach and, admittedly, much of what has gone out under her watch is borderline tacky. But what James has done in this regard will certainly make her family and herself secure for the future. And when all is said and done, it is ingrained in most creative people to make hay while the sun shines.

So in this sense, we all must cut E L James some slack. Because she is doing what we would all do if we were in her shoes.

Just keep a good thought the next time you're in a brick and mortar bookstore (yes, they still exist) or browsing the Internet. James' literary life was jumpstarted in this manner. She read millions of words before setting her own words down. As have all writers with a modicum of serious in their bones.

E L James is a part of the ever-growing pantheon of authors railing at the notion that people do not read anymore and that computer technology has blinded people to the joys of a physical book. Despite the dire predictions, people are still reading and while they are waiting for the next E L James book, they will most certainly be drawn to another title on the shelf. Maybe something *Fifty Shades* like. Maybe a biography. But guaranteed it will be something that will take them to a place that they want to be.

You are proof of that.

You are exhibit A.

Marc Shapiro 2012

BIBLIOGRAPHY
THE WRITER'S COFFEE SHOP

FIFTY SHADES OF GREY
Published in May 2011

FIFTY SHADES DARKER
Published in September 2011
FIFTY SHADES FREED
Published in January 2012

VINTAGE

FIFTY SHADES OF GREY
Published in April 2012 (digital and print)
FIFTY SHADES DARKER
Published in April 2012 (digital and print)
FIFTY SHADES FREED
Published in April 2012 (digital and print)

Marc Shapiro

DISCOGRAPHY
FIFTY SHADES OF GREY:
THE CLASSICAL ALBUM

THE MUSIC:
1. Lakme: Flower Duet 2. Bach: Adagio From Concerto No. 3 3. Villa-Lobos: Bachianas Brasileiras No. 5 4. Verdi: La Traviata Prelude 5. Pachelbe: Canon In D 6. Tallis: Spem In Alium 7. Chopin: Prelude No. 4 In E Minor 8. Rachmaninoff: Piano Concerto No. 2 9. Vaughan Williams: Fantasia On A Theme By Thomas Tallis 10. Canteloube: Chants d'Auvergne Bailero 11. Chopin: Nocturne No. 1 In B Flat Minor 12. Faure: Requiem In Paradisum 13: Bach: Goldberg Variation Aria 14. Debussy: La Fille Aux Cheveux De Lin 15. Bach: Jesu Joy Of Man's Desiring.

LISTEN TO THE SHADES

E L James put a lot of thought into creating the soundtracks for her *Fifty Shades* trilogy. Wide-ranging in her tastes, styles and influences, her mixture of classical music and pop tunes paints an aural tapestry that is a subtle adjunct to the words and emotions of the night and desire.

FIFTY SHADES OF GREY
THE MUSIC:

1. Lakme (Act 1) Flower Duet by Alain Lombard, Mady Mesple, Danielle Millet and The Orchestra Du Theatre National De Opera-Comique. 2. Sex On Fire by Kings Of Leon. 3. Adagio From Concerto No. 3 In D Minor by James Rhodes. 4. Misfit by Amy Studt. 5. I'm On Fire by Bruce Springsteen. 6. The Lightning Strike by Snow Patrol. 7. Heitor Villa Lobos: Bachianas Brasilas, Brasileiras No. 5 For Voice And Eight Cellos Aria by Ana Maria Martinez, Prague Philharmonia and Steven Mercurio. 8. Witchcraft by Frank Sinatra. 9. La Traviata Prelude by Italian Wedding Music. 10. Toxic by Britney Spears. 11. The Blower's Daughter by Damien Rice. 12. Canon And Gigue In D Major I Canon by English Concert And Trevor Pinnick. 13. Spem In Alium by Peter Phillips And The Tallis Scholars. 14. 24 Preludes Opus 28 No 4 In E Minor Largo by Alexandre Tharaud.

FIFTY SHADES DARKER
THE MUSIC:

1. What Is This Thing Called Love? by Ella Fitzgerald. 2. Like A Star by Corinne Bailey Rae. 3. Piano Concerto No. 2 In C Minor, Op, 18 Adagio Sostenuto by Helene Grimaud. 4. Lover You Should've Come Over by Jeff Buckley. 5. Principles Of Lust by Enigma. 6. Possession by Sarah McLachlan. 7. Try by Nelly Furtado. 8. The Scientist by Coldplay. 9. Every Breath You Take by The Police. 10. Heartbeats by Jose Gonzalez. 11. Homelands by Nitin Sawhney. 12. Fantasia On A Theme by Thomas Tallis by Andre Previn and The Royal Philharmonic Orchestra. 13. Chan Chan by The Buena Vista Social Club. 14. Crazy In Love by Beyonce. 15. I Put A Spell On You by Nina Simone. 16. Bailero (Chants d'Auvergne) 1st Series No. 2 by Academy Of St. Martin In The Fields, Edward Gardner and Kate Royal. 17. I've Got You Under My Skin by Michael Buble. 18. Come Fly With Me by Michael Buble. 19. Songbird by Eva Cassidy. 20. Nocturne No. 1 In B Flat Minor, Opus 9 No. 1 by Vladimir Ashkenazy. 21. Weather To Fly by Elbow. 22. King Of Pain by The Police. 23. Moondance by Van Morrison. 24. Someone Like You by Van Morrison. 25. This City Never Sleeps by The Eurythmics. 26. The First Time Ever I Saw Your Face by Roberta Flack.

FIFTY SHADES FREED
THE MUSIC:

1. You'll Never Find Another Love Like Mine by Michael Buble and Laura Pausini. 2. Wherever You Will Go by Charlene Soraia. 3. The Great Gig In The Sky by Pink Floyd. 4. Requiem, Opus 48 In Paradisum by Rachel Porter. 5. Wicked Game by Chris Isaak. 6. Goldberg Variations Aria By JS Bach by Glenn Gould. 7. I Say A Little Prayer by Aretha Franklin. 8. Walk On By by Aretha Franklin. 9. Sexy Bitch by David Guetta and Featuring Akon. 10. Touch Me by Rui Da Silva and Cassandra. 11. Sweet About Me by Gabriella Cilmi. 12. La Fille Aux Cheveux de Lin by Ronan O'Hora. 13. Jesu Joy Of Man's Desiring by Eteri Andjaparidze. 14. The Ugly Duckling by Danny Kaye.

A HISTORY OF EROTIC FICTION

Those arriving recently to erotic literature should be aware that the genre has a long and storied history of groundbreaking books that paved the way for *Fifty Shades of Grey*.

Scholars have long pointed to erotic fiction being an active and varied by-product as early on as the ancient world. "Song Of Songs" from The Old Testament, "Satyricon" and what many to this day consider the controversial and still regularly banned "Decameron" are prime early examples.

The 15th through 17th centuries saw the floodgates open to erotic literature. Conspicuous of the time and a telling example of how popular eroticism was in the old world was "The Tale Of Two Lovers" by Aeneas Sylvius Piccolomini. The book, written in 1444, would be the equivalent of a modern day best-seller throughout the 15th century. Author Piccolomini would later go on to greater and seemingly contradictory glory as Pope Pius II.

Such erotic forms as the "I Mod," an erotic mix of drawings and poetry, "The Whore's Rhetoric," "The School Of Venus," "A Dialogue Between A Married Woman And A Maid," and "The School Of Women" were among the high points in a period when eroticism was often dressed up in flowery language that did little to hide its true intent.

One work of the time that easily stands out was

"Sodom or The Quintessence of Debauchery," a play written by a radical fringe member of nobility, John Wilmot, the 2nd Earl of Rochester. The play emphasized anal sex as an attractive alternative to what was perceived as normal sexual intercourse.

This was the Wild West of erotic fiction. Lesser efforts and, for the time, classics of the day mixed easily in the public consciousness. They were vilified in many quarters but under the guise of puritanical attitudes, they were being sought out and read. The interest was proof that erotica would most certainly survive in some way, shape or form into the coming century and beyond.

The 18th century would prove a fruitful and diverse time for erotic fiction. The period was largely dominated by a series of light-hearted/flowery titles known as the Merryland Books. The Merryland Books were a strange excursion in which female and male body parts were described as the equivalent of a landscape painting. Among those titles were *The Present State of Bettyland* and *A New Description of Merryland*.

But it would remain for *Fanny Hill* by John Cleland to put the erotic novel on the map. The book (which has often gone under its intended full title *Fanny Hill: Memoirs of A Woman of Pleasure*) was controversial from its inception. Often the subject of censorship and available just as often in underground and pirated editions up until 1963 when the shackles of censorship were removed for good, *Fanny Hill* was worth its erotic reputation with outrageously graphic passages wrapped around regularly amusing moments. Destined to be a classic, *Fanny Hill* would be the high-water mark for erotica for some time to come.

During this period, the French, not surprisingly, were front and center in the world of erotica. Among the high points of the era were *The Lifted Curtain or Laura's Education* and *Dangerous Liaisons*.

By the end of the 18th century, erotica, and especially stories with the first hints of BDSM, were making their way into the world. A particular pioneer in this "new and different" world of sexuality came courtesy of the famous/infamous Marquis de Sade.

His seminal works, *Justine or The Misfortunes of Virtue* and *120 Days of Sodom*, with their upfront and largely unheard of accounts of sexual sadism and masochism, were, much like the fate of *Fanny Hill*, a center of controversy. The author, a born rebel who railed against seemingly all preconceived notions of normalcy, would spend time in jail and always in battle with what was perceived as the norm of the day.

Erotica emerged into the 19th century as both a legitimate and, yes, profitable form of literature. But, in a creative sense, much of the erotica of the period was less flowery, more direct and predictable and written by an assortment of pseudonyms, the likes of "Anonymous," "Ramrod" and "Rosa Coote." Erotica was being churned out like so much butter under such titles as *The Lustful Turk*, *My Lustful Adventures* and *Flossie: A Venus at Fifteen*. One of the more notorious efforts of the period was *Autobiography of a Flea* in which church higher-ups conspire to have sex with a recently deflowered virgin. Crude and rude for its day.

But the end of the century did play out against some interesting erotic moments. The S&M model of de Sade was picked up by several other authors who got around the subject matters of paganism, lesbianism and sadomasochism by way of a more cultured writing style. Typical of this new wave were the books *Venus in Furs* and *The Whippington Papers*. *Venus in Furs* was written by the Austrian Leopold von Sacher-Masoch, whose impact was so great that the growing popularity of the lifestyle would be named Masochism in honor of the author.

Things began getting legally complicated for the quite prolific English publishing industry of the day. By the end of the 19th century, many of the top-flight publishers uprooted and moved their base of operations to a more liberal Paris, where the genre continued to flourish, albeit in rather graphic and base manner; as witness such titles of the period as *Raped on the Railway: A True Story of a Lady Who Was First Ravished and Then Flagellated on the Scotch Express* and *The Memoirs of Dolly Morton*.

Heading into the 20th century, much of erotica remained in a rather pornographic place. But the future for quality erotica looked bright.

Writers of legitimate talent and culture were, either by design or the reality of making a living, suddenly quick to add their own elements of erotic nature to their novels. The veil of "hack" was being lifted to reveal a renaissance of top-flight writing containing real characters and believable emotion.

A steady stream of books, attributed to Anonymous but reportedly the work of no less a talent than George Reginald Bacchus, included *The Confessions of Nemesis Hunt*, *The Way of a Man With A Maid* and *Pleasure Bound Afloat* and received high marks. Other superior erotic works of the time were *Josephine Mutzenbacher* by Felix Salten, *Sadopaideia* by Anonymous (but attributed to Algernon Swinburne) and *Les Memoires d'un jeune Don Juan* by Guillaume Apollinaire.

The 19th century would conclude with erotic fiction on the upswing. Authors with a wider worldview than mere titillation were abroad in the world of erotica, perceived as men and women of letters rather than back-alley hacks. It was a time of growth for the form.

Beginning in the late-1920s, more authors emerged whose works remain literary classics with timeless tales containing erotic elements. Admittedly, timing had a lot to do with this mid to late 20th century resurgence. The world was coming to embrace the avant-garde in all its many forms and, by association, eroticism was considered legitimate artistic expression.

High on this list were the works of Henry Miller, whose books *Tropic of Cancer* and *Tropic of Capricorn* remain a majestic tour of the human spirit and psyche set in often erotic tableaus. *The Story of O* by Pauline Reage was very much in the harsher areas of eroticism and, in many ways, could be considered a forerunner of the *Fifty Shades* books in its education of a young innocent who comes to the dark side of sexuality.

Vladimir Nabokov, with his classic *Lolita* and the equally taut *Ardor*, blurred the lines even further. His stories most certainly had their tantalizing moments but, as couched within traditional elements of literary storytelling, they have often been the topic of considerable debate by observers of the literary scene.

Anais Nin has made a strong case for the distaff

side of erotic storytelling with a *Delta of Venus* and *Little Birds* and her journals.These were the titles that ultimately kicked open the critical door. Books with elements of erotica were suddenly being considered in a more respectful manner and judged as legitimate, albeit still off and away from the mainstream forms of literature.

Into the present, erotic fiction has risen to a level of respectability in many quarters, garnering its own section in bookstores, occasionally marked as erotica but more often than not as literary. We see various shades and colors of erotica in the mass-market paperback romance novels, and in the more extreme works by the likes of Anne Rice and others who make regular appearances on the best-seller lists. And with the success of *Fifty Shades of Grey*, the literary world is exploding with endless books, admittedly of varying quality, that are finding intimate moments done up in intimate detail, an adjunct to storytelling.

Like its predecessors, *Fifty Shades* is successful because people want to read these often explicit tales.

As history shows, this has always been the case.

Marc Shapiro

CINEMA EROTIC

It goes without saying that nearly everybody in the known universe is waiting anxiously for *Fifty Shades of Grey* to hit the big screen. But while you are waiting, there is a literal library of erotically charged films to revisit, admire and get you in the proper mood.

THE STORY OF O
(1975)DIRECTOR: Just JaeckinSTARS: Corinne Clery, Udo Kier, Anthony SteeleThe setup of this dated yet still effective journey into sexual perversion is simple. O is taken to an isolated manor where she is forced into being a victim of sexual dominance and sadomasochism to prove her love to her boyfriend. The scenes of sexual dominance by masked men and the whippings and other elements of humiliation are still fairly powerful and grim but better than average acting plus the director's adherence to a soft, almost gauze-like approach to filming makes this film one of those underappreciated classics that, to this day, has critics on both sides of *The Story of O* taking sides.

LAST TANGO IN PARIS
(1972)DIRECTOR: Bernardo BertolucciCAST: Marlon Brando, Maria SchneiderThe sex is very primal and often borders on abuse and brutality. The agreement between grieving widower Paul and young

innocent Jeannie to have sex and nothing more is seemingly cut roughly from a classic BDSM role. All of which made *Last Tango In Paris* a headline-grabbing NC-17 film upon its initial release. But eventually people got around to seeing that the film actually told a powerful tale of two lost souls in crisis. Brando, who was notorious for giving solid performances in bad films, takes the emotionally tortured Paul to his heart and is constantly believable in his pain and anguish. Newcomer Schneider, admittedly someone with limited acting skills, managed a quietly strong performance as someone who must choose at the crossroads of life. Watch for the sex, which is nothing if not erotic. Stay for the story.

9 1/2 WEEKS

(1986)DIRECTOR: Adrian LyneCAST: Mickey Rourke, Kim BasingerThe basic setup is good. Art gallery worker meets a mysterious stranger and embarks on a prolonged sexual romp (hence the title). The film skirts the notion of a BDSM theme, although the Mickey Rourke character appears to be definitely in charge. The sex scenes, in various indoor and outdoor locations, are appropriately hot and occasionally kinky. Of particular note is the scene where Kim Basinger's character pleasures herself in a darkened room. A well-filmed and truly explicit outing. The storyline is occasionally muddled but that does not really detract from the film's lingering notoriety which, on an erotic level, is richly deserved.

SECRETARY

(2002)DIRECTOR: Steven ShainbergCAST: James Spader, Maggie GyllenhaalIf you could pin E L James down, my guess is that she saw this movie at least once in preparation for writing *Fifty Shades of Grey*. And I'm not just talking about the pure coincidence that James Spader's control freak lawyer is named Mr. Grey. This is erotic/BDSM light. A woman recently released from a mental institution goes to work for the stuffy Mr. Grey. Along the way she comes to know and, by degrees, appreciate her employer's masochistic ways. A solid effort played as much for subtle humor as drama. There are a handful of relatively soft dominant/submissive moments, none of which comes across as really serious business. The story, typical of big studio efforts, has a more upbeat and, dare we say, conventional conclusion. Yes, there was probably a much tougher story to be told here and, perhaps someday, somebody will. Mild titillation to be sure. But surprisingly effective.

CRASH

(1996)DIRECTOR: David Cronenberg CAST: James Spader, Holly Hunter, Elias Koteas, Deborah Kara UngerEasily one of the most bleak and disturbing exercises in kinky erotic ever put to film. A young couple with a decidedly different open marriage have their world turned upside down when the husband, following a near fatal auto accident, is drawn to the female survivor, a woman who now must go through life a mass of scars and metal braces. The connection is immediate and it is not long before the couple are having sex in, where else, the backseat of a car. The ties between sex and cars is further explored when the married couple and the husband's new mistress are drawn to a secret society of car crash survivors who draw sexual energy from the re-creation of car crashes. There is a lot of sex but done up in ways that sends up the inherent power of metal machinery as it does the eroticism of sex. At its darkest and, in Cronenberg's hands most deliberate, *Crash* teeters precariously close to being pure porn of a particularly dastardly variety. But those brave enough to take the complete ride (and not walk out like many did when the film was first released) will find a rough, raw burn of a story that, in the time-honored tradition of solid scripting, will make perfect sense.

EMMANUELLE

(1974)DIRECTOR: Just JaeckinCAST: Sylvia Kristel, Alain Cuny, Marika GreenWhile the lion's share of director Just Jaeckin's notoriety centers around *The Story of O*, his previous erotic adventure, *Emmanuelle*, is easily as enticing and offers a leisurely, if no less erotic, travelogue of a young girl's sexual awakening in and around the jungles of Thailand. The title character is happily married to a much older and understanding man. They have an open marriage and so, when opportunity presents itself in the form of a female traveling companion, Emmanuelle is off on a nonstop sexual adventure that takes her into various avenues of sexuality including lesbianism and encounters with proper male strangers. There is nothing forced or savage in these encounters. Everything is free and easy and, as photographed through a soft fuzzy lens, discreet and, for the most part, respectful. Very much a by-product of emerging erotic freedom in the '70s, *Emmanuelle* has stood the test of time.

IN THE REALM OF THE SENSES

(1976)DIRECTOR: Nagisa OshimaCAST: Tatsuya Fuji, Eiko Matsuda, Aoi NakajimaThis Japanese film, reportedly based on a true story, has the distinction of being banned at one time or another in just about every country on the planet. Almost impossible to find now, but if you do come across a copy, be prepared for a psychosexual journey into erotica and obsession that is conspicuous by its bleakness and discomfort level. A man and a woman begin a sexual affair that is so extreme and addictive that it literally brings them to a level of insanity. There is sex, lots of it that walks a very uneasy line between erotica and unadulterated pornography and reflects the couple's slow but steady descent into madness. One that eventually turns to the darkest shades of death and mutilation. This movie is unapologetically grim. But it is also quite daring in content and execution. *In The Realm of The Senses* is the polar opposite of the soft and fuzzy erotic film. It is quite literally a sexual journey into hell.

SOURCES

I would like to thank the following people who supplied interviews and insights into the *Fifty Shades*/E L James story: Tish Beaty, former editor and acquisitions manager at The Writer's Coffee Shop. Jenny Pedroza, marketing director of The Writer's Coffee Shop. Jessica Donaghy, features editor of the website Goodreads.

NEWSPAPERS

The London Daily Mail, The London Evening Standard, Chicago Tribune, Times Of India, Irish Central, The New York Observer, UT San Diego, The Hartford Courant, The Telegraph, Shoreline Times, The Guardian, The Sydney Morning Herald, The Star Telegram, USA Today, Los Angeles Times, The Herald Sun, Columbus Dispatch, Express And Star, Daily Record, Oklahoma Daily, New York Times, Wall Street Journal, New York Post, The Australian, The Sunday Times, The Vancouver Sun, International Business Times.

MAGAZINES

Woman And Home, People, Publishers Weekly, Entertainment Weekly, Newsday, GQ .

WEBSITES

The Writer's Coffee Shop, Goodreads, Entertainmentwise, stuff.co.nz, Face The Facts, Rachael Wade, Fiction Vixen, boston.com, Bona Fide Reflections, miami.com, My Secret Romance, Pop Culture Junkies, fanfiction.net, Crushable, Awesomeness, Hollywood Life, The Pattinson Post, Life Between Pages, Regan Walsh, Bookish Temptations, Red Carpet News, Tongue Twied, True Twihard 4 Ever, Page Daily, Dear Author, Galley Cat, Lara's Book Club, TVNZ, Oh Fifty, Book That Thing, All About You, Guilty Pleasures, Sinful Books, Celebrity Net Worth, Perez-Hilton, Deadline.com, The Examiner, newJersey.com, Celebuzz, London Guru, Entertainment And Stars, Screen Crush, Gossip Cop, Carlsbad Patch, Harrison Patch, Vulture

RADIO, TELEVISION AND MISCELLANEOUS

National Public Radio, U.S. book tour quotes and transcripts, Access Hollywood, CBC Radio, 20/20, Today, CNN, Associated Press, CBS News, E L James official website, 720 Sydney, 9 News, MTV, The View, X17, IMDB.

BOOKS

A History of Erotic Literature by Patrick Kearney
A History of Pornography by H. Montgomery Hyde

For more books by Marc Shapiro visit

We Love Jenni: The Unauthorized Biography of Jenni Rivera with Charlie Vazquez
https://riverdaleavebooks.com/books/28/we-love-jenni-an-unauthorized-biography

Who Is Katie Holmes?:_An Unauthorized Biography
https://riverdaleavebooks.com/books/33/who-is-katie-holmes-an-unauthorized-biography

Legally Bieber: Justin Bieber at 18
An Unauthorized Biography
http://riverdaleavebooks.com/books/41/legally-bieber-justin-bieber-at-18

Annette Funicello: America's Sweetheart
An Unauthorized Biography
http://riverdaleavebooks.com/books/44/annette-funicello-americas-sweetheart

Game: The Resurrection of Tim Tebow
An Unauthorized Biography
http://riverdaleavebooks.com/books/3084/game-the-resurrection-of-tim-tebow

Lorde: Your Heroine
How This Young Feminist Broke the Rules and Succeeded
http://riverdaleavebooks.com/books/4113/lorde-your-heroine-how-this-young-feminist-broke-the-rules-and-succeeded

19610236R00114

Printed in Poland
by Amazon Fulfillment
Poland Sp. z o.o., Wrocław